JENA 1800

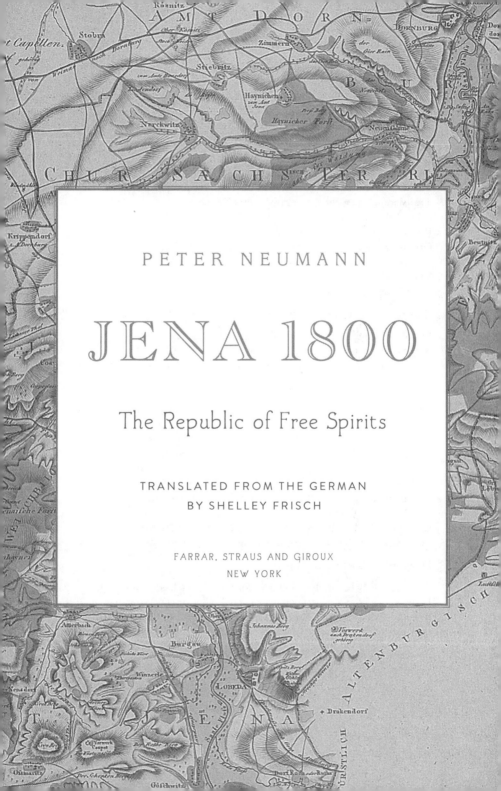

PETER NEUMANN

JENA 1800

The Republic of Free Spirits

TRANSLATED FROM THE GERMAN
BY SHELLEY FRISCH

FARRAR, STRAUS AND GIROUX
NEW YORK

Farrar, Straus and Giroux
120 Broadway, New York 10271

Illustration credits can be found on pages 243–244.

Library of Congress Cataloging-in-Publication Data
Names: Neumann, Peter, 1987– author. | Frisch, Shelley Laura, translator.
Title: Jena 1800 : the republic of free spirits / Peter Neumann ; translated
    from the German by Shelley Frisch.
Other titles: Jena 1800. English | Jena eighteen hundred
Description: First American edition. | New York : Farrar, Straus and
    Giroux, 2022. | "Originally published in German in 2018 by Siedler
    Verlag, Germany" | Includes bibliographical references and index.
Identifiers: LCCN 2021025281 | ISBN 9780374178697 (hardcover)
Subjects: LCSH: Romanticism—Germany. | German literature—
    19th century—History and criticism. | Philosophy, German—
    19th century. | Jena (Germany)—Intellectual life—19th century. |
    LCGFT: Literary criticism.
Classification: LCC PT363.P5 N4913 2022 | DDC 830.9/006—dc23
LC record available at https://lccn.loc.gov/2021025281

Designed by Janet Evans-Scanlon

Our books may be purchased in bulk for promotional, educational, or
business use. Please contact your local bookseller or the Macmillan
Corporate and Premium Sales Department at 1-800-221-7945, extension
5442, or by email at MacmillanSpecialMarkets@macmillan.com.

www.fsgbooks.com
www.twitter.com/fsgbooks • www.facebook.com/fsgbooks

10 9 8 7 6 5 4 3 2 1

Contents

CONTENTS

JENA 1800

The Morning After

The earth shuddered and the windowpanes clattered as muffled yet unmistakable cannon booms reverberated throughout the city. The attack was coming from the south. An overpowering blast was followed by a weaker one, and then, little by little, the staccato blasts escalated into a constant roar, as though entire batteries were being shot off. The Prussian outposts at Maua and Winzerla had already been captured, and the other troops had retreated to the north.

People lay on their beds, fully clad and alert. The dead silence in the city could be shattered at any moment by a fire alarm or clanging bells. Most residents stayed in their homes, quietly peeking out from time to time and listening fearfully for what might lie ahead.

Shots from French patrol units would soon echo through the narrow streets, and the townspeople would be exposed to a whole new world, to scenes they would never have thought possible. Students used to hearing lectures about logic and metaphysics, debating the merits of one philosophical system or another, and discussing literature, art, history, and the philosophy of nature, awoke to the sounds and sights of famished, torch-bearing soldiers prowling the streets in the early morning hours on October 13, 1806. Only those who kept their composure, had a reasonably good command of French, and refrained from hostile action would be spared the pillage and looting. Even so, jeering and rampaging filled the air. Most of the houses had been looted by ten in the morning: money, gold watches, silverware were gone. Wine, too—and there was more than enough wine in the area. *Ouvrez la porte!* All who did not comply voluntarily had their doors pried open on the spot. The people knew not to open their shutters. The soldiers stopped at nothing, and would smash windows to gain access; they simply hoisted themselves up, and in they went.

By noon, accompanied by military marches and headed up by generals and officers crowned with tall plumes, stately and elegant, the first regular troops had moved in through the Neutor in the south and begun to restore order. As the streets grew calm again, the local ragpickers, riffraff, and con artists laid claim to anything the French left behind in the houses. But this sense of calm was deceptive. At a time of uncertainty and fear, with world history and world spirit on a collision course, there was no telling how things would develop. War was in the air. And war would come indeed. All would be decided in Jena.

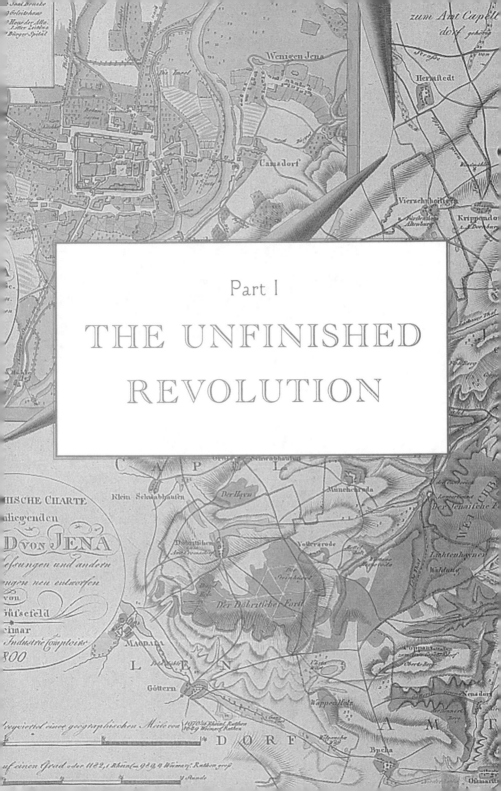

Part I

THE UNFINISHED
REVOLUTION

A Philosophy Takes the Continent by Storm

It was early evening. Normally, all the residents of Leutragasse 5 spent many hours secluded in their rooms, working and writing, but as the day drew to a close, the brothers Friedrich ("Fritz") and August Wilhelm Schlegel ("Wilhelm"), Caroline Schlegel, Dorothea Veit, Friedrich Wilhelm Joseph Schelling, Friedrich von Hardenberg ("Novalis"), and Ludwig Tieck gathered around the small sofa in the parlor, right next to the stove. Tea was served, along with cheese, pickled herring, and potatoes, all leftovers from lunch. Schelling kept reaching into the pickle jar. The household savings were nearly depleted; not much money was flowing in from the occupants' writing. But financial matters were of lesser importance to them that night; they dined, philosophized, and studied Italian. That evening, Dante was on the agenda, *La Divina Commedia*, in which Fritz was well versed. When he recited Dante, his eyes lit up; his well-proportioned facial features, of late generally strained and furrowed as he struggled to make progress on the second part of his novel *Lucinde*, relaxed and smoothed out. While reciting, he practically forgot about the need to eat.

While *Lucinde* awaited its continuation—the first part had been published half a year earlier, at Eastertime in 1799—

Schelling labored over a long poem about nature. He set out to write the most poetic of all poems, one with no quality more particular than that, or at least nothing that stood out as *particular*; he was aiming for a singular, didactic poem, a speculative epic, with absolute form as its only content. He worked on it in solitude. But this was Jena, and Jena was too small for someone to get lost in his own thoughts and go unnoticed. Everyone there knew what Schelling was up to.

His *First Outline of a System of the Philosophy of Nature* had recently been published, and Schelling's name was on everybody's lips. The publication had been fiercely attacked in literary journals, while the students in Jena lay at his feet. Schelling rubbed people the wrong way, mostly kept to himself, and remained an enigma even to his friends. Watching him eat his soup at lunchtime, bent over the table, one might easily imagine he was a military commander, perhaps a French general, but not a great philosopher. Schelling didn't quite fit into the world of teaching, nor was he a good match for the literary sphere. Caroline came to describe him as "true granite."

Caroline was the one person receptive to his nature. She was quite taken with him, and he with her, although she was almost twelve years his senior. Just recently, in secret, he had dazzled her by slipping a black feather onto her hat. A black feather signified enchantment, magic, mystery. Schelling flirted with her so shamelessly, right in front of the group, that Novalis, observing the spectacle out of the corner of his eye, saw the pitch-black storm clouds of a scandal forming. Something about him fascinated her—perhaps his aloofness, perhaps his originality. When they were together, a quarrel would ensue in no more than six minutes. He was far and away the most interesting person she had come across since August Wilhelm Schlegel—that is, Wilhelm, her husband.

Wilhelm and Caroline, as was well known around town and at home, took a dim view of the holy sacrament of marriage. They lived together more like good friends than people who had promised to be faithful to each other forever. By this point their marriage was evidently only on paper. Caroline didn't care what the townspeople were saying. They could gossip all they wanted; she was used to it.

Caroline played the poised hostess while Schelling beguiled her and Wilhelm flirted with Dorothea, who lived with his brother Fritz. It was all a big jumble. Tieck, for one, considered the whole thing a complete farce. But no one wanted to say a word about it, including Tieck himself. With the world around them caving in a little bit more with each passing day, they needed to stick together at least there, in their inner circle.

The revolution was over; Napoleon Bonaparte had ended it. By means of a clever coup he had propelled himself to the top of the fledgling republic, and now, as first consul in Paris, he wielded power throughout France. The Ancien Régime was a thing of the past. Pius VI, the pope in Rome, had breathed his last; held prisoner in the citadel of Valence since February 1798, when French troops occupied the Papal States, he died there in captivity. Without a doubt, a turning point had arrived. The power of the papacy, which had maintained stability in Europe over the course of centuries, had come to an end. Never had the future been so uncertain; it seemed invariably consigned to the past before it even arrived. Time had been divided into a before and an after.

The ruling class was also on the alert, fearing that all this democratic fervor could spill over from the students to the common people and artisans, then to the farmers, servants, and day laborers. In Paris, the populace had laid down its own laws and liberated itself from the class that had kept it in shackles, and its extremes in doing so extended even to public executions.

The duke in Weimar kept an eagle eye on which scholar was giving what lecture, which course materials were circulating, and what was making its way to the public—and how it was getting there. Weimar was tightening the reins on the much-vaunted intellectual freedom in Jena. Even the slightest attempt to make common cause with the revolution was met with prosecution. The philosopher Johann Gottlieb Fichte had just been dismissed from the university that summer on a trumped-up charge of "atheism," which was a mere pretext. Fichte had been a thorn in the duke's side from the outset, even back when the duke and Johann Wolfgang von Goethe had been in the vicinity of Mainz—which was occupied by the French—discussing Fichte's initial appointment to Jena. Fichte was regarded as Immanuel Kant's intellectual heir, yet he was also considered a sympathizer with the French Revolution.

These were only some of the disputes that were electrifying the duchy of Saxe-Weimar in November 1799. *Freedom* was a watchword of these days, as was *autonomy*. The only thing missing was a viable foundation to build on. The events in Paris had made it amply clear that brute force did not lead to the desired result. The revolution devoured its young and then collapsed, but what freedom could be greater than freedom of thought and of art? Philosophy and literature could take the place of political actionism and revolutionary ballyhoo. The complex path to the long-desired political freedom would entail philosophical reflection and poetic imagination, which alone could bridge the divide between freedom and nature, and pave the way to a still utterly unspecified era. The new century was looming, and there was no going back. In Paris, the revolution was over and done with, but in Jena it was just getting started.

In November 1799, Jena was essentially the intellectual and cultural center of Germany. Home to fewer than five thousand residents, almost a fifth of them students, it was a midsized university town, an industrial and commercial city in the duchy of Saxe-Weimar, set in a valley between steep limestone cliffs. Its medieval buildings barely reached beyond the old city limits. In the north were the sunny mountain slopes where grapes, used to make full-bodied wine in autumn, grew among ruined castles; to the south lay expanses of land adjoining the water where students could enjoy a good swim during the summer. Everyone knew one another. The Leutra River snaked along the gardens outside the city walls, a thin silver thread that was channeled through the narrow alleys twice a week, carrying off household refuse and the contents of the chamber pots that were dumped out the windows onto the streets in the early morning hours, and eventually pouring into the Saale River.

The "Salana," originally established in 1558 in a former Dominican monastery, was set up as a replacement for the university in Wittenberg; eleven years earlier, during the Schmalkaldic War, the military alliance of Lutheran princes within the Holy Roman Empire had capitulated to the imperial forces of Charles V, leaving Wittenberg on foreign territory. To all appearances, Jena was a German provincial backwater, a parochial place with a populace made up of students, professors, and philistines. The three major east-west streets—Johannisgasse to the north, Kollegiengasse to the south, and Leutragasse between them—were dotted with highly impressive buildings, many of them professors' residences that were half scholarly apartment and half lecture hall, and were handed down through generations. In between those main streets, however, the atmosphere was stultifying. While neighboring Weimar, the dowager duchess Anna Amalia's Musenhof (courtyard of the muses), lay on a plateau and was open on all sides, in Jena everything bumped up against everything else. Sunlight never reached farther down than the top floors. Some pointed gables bent backward, while others tipped forward menacingly.

In contrast to the faculty, the students were forbidden to live outside the city walls, which made conditions all the more cramped, confining, and airless. Nothing could be done about the greasy walls, the bedbugs that settled in the mattresses. Yet this town enticed everyone who was anyone, and those who aspired to attain such special distinction. In the last decade of the eighteenth century, word spread throughout Europe that this town was the true heart of European intellectual life. Plato's Academy could now be found on the Saale River.

Fichte, a fervent supporter of the new critical philosophy, had been in Jena since 1794. Thirteen years earlier, Kant had triggered a philosophical earthquake from his hometown of Königsberg. The *Critique of Pure Reason*, published in Riga in 1781, was *the* work of the day. Kant aimed to place philosophy on a secure foundation. What we learn about objects, he explained, depends on the forms of our understanding and the forms of our perception, and the forms of our intuition are space and time. We can know nothing about how things in themselves actually are, Kant contended; the scope of our knowledge is limited.

Kant's critique of reason shook the intellectual world. From that time forward, all metaphysical proofs of the existence of God were rendered hopelessly out of date. God's existence could be neither confirmed nor refuted. The only thing that could be said with certainty in regard to the fundamental questions of metaphysics—world, soul, God, freedom, and immortality—was that no amount of questioning would yield an answer. Moses Mendelssohn, a philosopher who had been following the events from Berlin in the early 1780s, called Kant the "all-crusher."

Even so, the book initially gathered dust on bookstore shelves. Only in Jena, later in the decade, did it receive the attention it merited; it was read, discussed, and commented on, and that—concurrently with the major revolution unfolding a few hundred miles away in Paris—was the beginning of its triumphant advance across the continent.

The new critical thinking seized the European continent like a shockwave, plunging the intelligentsia into a deep crisis, and the only way to emerge from this crisis was to free oneself. *Sapere aude* (dare to know)—"Have the courage to use your *own* understanding"—was Kant's maxim. No educated person could escape doing so. There were no longer oases of eternal truths, nor was there refuge in the seclusion of venerable universities. Over in Paris, it had been the political, actual revolution that transformed the city, whereas in Jena it was the philosophical revolution of ideas that turned everything upside down. The old belief systems no longer held. Kant was the new era, and Fichte its messiah.

Since Fichte had come to Jena, students flocked in from all directions: Norway, Sweden, Switzerland, Hungary, Greece—and those from France had either fled the land of the revolution or wanted to continue developing revolutionary ideas, having identified Fichte as the theorist of political freedom. Man has no authority above himself, Fichte insisted, and must adhere only to laws that he, as a rational being, has enacted for himself.

Fichte had become famous overnight with a treatise on

religion. Readers assumed that this treatise was in fact Kant's missing fourth critique. Four questions, Kant said, mark the field of philosophy: What can I know? What ought I to do? What may I hope for? What is man? For all intents and purposes, there was actually only a single question, because the first three questions were subsumed in the last. With his three critiques, then, Kant had defined what the field of philosophy could achieve, and had commented on epistemological, moral, aesthetic, and other elements. On the path to establishing a solid foundation for philosophy, he had outlined the potential and limits of human knowledge, developed an approach to ethics from the principles of pure reason, and explained why man—a creature both sensual and intellectual—could have any degree of freedom, even though the world could only be thought of as governed by necessity and natural laws. Up to that point, however, Kant had not taken a stand on questions of religion or the nature of hope.

It seemed to readers that *Attempt at a Critique of All Revelation*, which was published anonymously, just had to be the concluding volume of the critical enterprise. This conclusion was not far-fetched; Fichte believed that his thinking was totally in line with Kant's. His reverence for Kant was so great that when he and his wife, Johanna, had a son, they did not hesitate to name him Immanuel: Immanuel Hermann, to be precise. Fichte staunchly insisted that little Immanuel was the spitting image of his great eponym. Fichte was eventually revealed to be the author of the *Attempt* and was appointed to the university as a result of Goethe's advocacy with the duke back in Mainz.

That fall, Friedrich Schiller could be seen hurrying through the streets in a blue tailcoat, red neckerchief, yellow trousers, and dark stockings, when he was not confined to his bed by yet another bout of the illness that racked him with spasms and made it virtually impossible for him to leave the house. The time had passed when he had to fight his way through crowds; the days when his public appearance set the whole city in an uproar were over.

He had yet to make a full recovery from driving himself nearly to collapse almost eight years earlier, yet he was as hard at work as ever. He had just completed a trilogy, *Wallenstein*, a monumental drama about the Thirty Years' War. When Goethe came to Jena for a visit, he invariably spent time at his colleague's home. Schiller had widened the driveway in front of the garden house where he spent the summer months, and often well into October or even November, for the sole purpose of accommodating Goethe's carriage—the *Fahrhäuschen* (little house on wheels), as Goethe was fond of calling it. The two of them pondered poetry and philosophy, natural science and politics. And now there were even plans afoot, supported by the duke, for Schiller to relocate. Schiller wanted to be in Weimar, as near as possible to the theater and to his friend.

Schiller had come to Jena long before Fichte. Just a few short weeks before the storming of the Bastille, which marked the onset of the French Revolution, Schiller had delivered his inaugural lecture on two consecutive evenings in the city where he was now living with his wife, Charlotte, known as Lolo, and the children. The Griesbach Auditorium—the largest in the city, with a seating capacity of four hundred—was jam-packed on both nights.

Schiller had also studied Kant, particularly his *Critique of Judgment*, which was published in 1790. The free harmonious play of the cognitive faculties that Kant described in that work became the focus of Schiller's thinking about the aesthetic education of man, how imagination and understanding interact in aesthetic intuition, and how a concept has to dance around intuition in order to encompass it. Schiller was convinced that art liberated man from the rule of mere conceptualized thinking, and shattered the shackles of blind necessity. For Schiller, man was truly free only when at play.

In Jena, Kant was omnipresent. Kantianism had become quite the sensation. Students tossed around concepts they knew little about, constructing systems while brandishing their swords in a childish display. Their bold philosophical constructions were sure to collapse at the slightest whiff of criticism; their mind games, which amounted to speculative, convoluted propositions, led nowhere. Joining in was all that mattered. Students in all disciplines gravitated to the philosophers. Who could care about following a tiresome curriculum if you could spiral up into the stratosphere of the mind with Kant, Fichte, and Schiller?

And in the past year, a new professor, Schelling, had joined the faculty. His critical thinking was even more radical than that of his predecessors, guided by the principle that philosophical inquiry was still far from its endpoint. He considered it utterly misguided to exclude the fundamental questions of metaphysics from critical thinking. The results were in place, Schelling argued in a letter to his friend Georg Wilhelm Friedrich Hegel, but the premises were still lacking.

Schelling's reputation had preceded him. Before beginning his Jena lectureship, he had spent the summer in Dresden in the company of the two Schlegel brothers, Wilhelm and Fritz, as well as with Caroline, Novalis, and Fichte; there, he had already been well on his way to taking his place on the throne of critical philosophy. No sooner had he arrived in Jena than he turned everything upside down.

Venturing into Freedom

MADAME BÖHMER DIPS HER TOE
INTO THE REVOLUTION

She was the object of a great many whispered remarks on the streets in Jena as she strolled across the market on Tuesdays, Thursdays, and Saturdays, while the countrywomen (who did not pay her any mind) waited for customers at their baskets, carts, and kiosks, their voices booming across the square: *Fresh fruit! Fresh vegetables!* The word was that Caroline Schlegel, at the side of the famous naturalist and travel writer Georg Forster, had been in cahoots with the Jacobins back in Mainz when the city, conquered by French revolutionary troops, had been summarily proclaimed a republic. It had been a revolution from below, creating the first republic on German soil.

The time Caroline spent in Mainz had left its mark on her. She had experienced firsthand what it meant to go from enthusiastic but uninvolved observer of the revolution to persecuted partisan. She could pinpoint the moment when her own life was thrown off course, triggering a terrible sequence of events and putting everything at stake. She knew what it felt like to be dragged into an abyss, with only the helping hand of a friend to pull her back out. Her changing set of names attested to the

twisting path of her destiny: she was Dorothea Caroline Alber-
tine, née Michaelis, widow of Johann Böhmer, remarried to
Wilhelm Schlegel.

In Jena, Caroline was still regarded as the "famous Mme.
Böhmer" who had done time at the prison fortress Königstein as
a member of the Jacobin Club. She was eyed with suspicion and
treated like an outcast by many, in particular by Karl August Böttiger, the ambitious journalist from Weimar, who always kept
an eye out for gossip. Just recently she had heard two women
chatting at the market while she was trying on a wide-brimmed
hat. (It looked good on her; Schelling was sure to be pleased.)
She watched the two women out of the corner of her eye as
she gazed in the mirror and saw them pointing their fingers at
her behind her back. In a small town like this, idle chatter was
unavoidable.

Whenever Caroline heard the name Königstein, what flashed
though her mind were the horrors of the days when she was held
captive at the fortress in Taunus following her failed attempt, in
April 1793, to escape from Mainz to her friends, the Gotters, in
Gotha. Just a few miles past Oppenheim, southeast from Mainz,
at a Prussian outpost, she had been stopped, searched, and—
after a quick look at her passport—brought to headquarters in
Frankfurt. The name Böhmer was known to the authorities.
Caroline's brother-in-law, Georg Wilhelm Böhmer, had worked
closely with General Adam-Philippe de Custine, a leader in the
French Revolution. *Odious democrats.* Her luggage was confiscated,
and from headquarters she went straight into detention. Rather
than liberty trees planted during the revolutionary period, she
faced the walls of a dark cell.

Once, she had envisioned Mainz as the site of a long-yearned-
for change of pace from her overly constrained early life. Johann

David Michaelis, her father, was a highly respected theologian and orientialist at the venerable University of Göttingen, a stronghold of the German Enlightenment. Goethe would have loved to study with Michaelis in Göttingen. Her father lived in one of the most opulent buildings in the city, on Prinzenstrasse, right across the street from the main academic building and the university library. Caroline grew up in this academic setting, in the company of all her father's esteemed guests, an environment in which it was always essential to adhere to proper etiquette.

Shortly before her twenty-first birthday, Caroline was married to Johann Franz Wilhelm Böhmer, a public health officer and mountain doctor ten years her senior, and she followed him to Clausthal in the Upper Harz region of central Germany. One year later, in 1785, their daughter, Auguste ("Gustel"), was born. The spouses shared a bond of friendship and devotion. Caroline put aside her own spirit of discovery, and they lived by clearly defined rules.

Four years after the wedding, her husband died of an infection. By this time, they had a second child, Therese, and another was on the way. Caroline felt that her only option was to return to Göttingen. It seemed ill-advised, but what was the point of remaining in Clausthal, which offered little more in the way of education than practical courses for miners and ironworkers?

She did not have much time to think things over. First came the death of her son, Wilhelm, just a few weeks after his birth; then Therese died. When her father died as well, she made the decision to go to Mainz. With her back to the wall, there was no choice but to charge ahead.

She knew a few people in Mainz, including Georg Forster, who held an appointment as head librarian at the university there, and Forster's wife, Therese Heyne, the daughter of the classicist Christian Gottlob Heyne. In Göttingen, she and Meta Forkel, Dorothea Schlözer, and Philippine Engelhardt had formed a group of professors' daughters who wrote essays and poems and longed to become actively involved in academic and literary activities. They focused on escaping their cramped surroundings, avoiding all the deplorable tea parties, and moving on to other delights: French, English, Italian, Diderot, Shakespeare, Goldoni! Caroline knew of Forster's republican outlook, but when she left Göttingen, she had no idea of the dangers ahead in Mainz. Rebellion was in; decorum was out.

She never thought it possible that her venture into freedom could culminate in captivity and preventive detention. She had hoped to be invigorated by the war, if it should come; she anticipated that it would bring about a rejuvenation of her ossifed era. Caroline wanted to be able to tell her grandchildren about experiencing a siege, about a religious man having his long nose lopped off on the town square.

She was almost glad to have Auguste with her in the prison. Although Gustel was still a child, Caroline could confide in her when she didn't know how to go on. And that was the case more often than she would have wished. The conditions in Königstein were abysmal. One cell held seven inmates. On top of that, Caroline was pregnant—not by Forster, even though Therese and half the world alleged that she had had a relationship with him. The truth was actually far worse: the father of this baby was a young French officer of the occupying forces, the nephew and adjutant of General François Ignace Ervoil d'Oyre, who had now taken the helm from Custine. And while from a distance she heard the roar of the cannons of the Holy Roman Empire's artillery, she cursed how recklessly she had behaved during the heady celebrations of freedom on the day of the conquest.

Caroline did not feel the least bit guilty; there was no truth to the accusations of collaboration with the French that had been leveled against her. If she had done what she was being reproached for, she would have owned up to it. But she never would have exposed Auguste to such danger. She could not expect support of any kind from Forster, who had now landed in Paris. Caroline regarded herself as a political hostage.

The days in the prison were long. Caroline felt that time was coming to an absolute standstill. She had witnessed too much: horrid scenes of inmates beaten to death without so much as an interrogation, let alone a trial. At one point she did not leave her bed for three weeks. But Gustel was there. Caroline would have to go on for her sake.

In despair, she pinned her hopes on being released, but no one was prepared to post her bail. Even Goethe, the influential privy councilor and minister, whom she had once joyfully welcomed to her parents' home in Göttingen and whom she had seen again the previous August in Mainz—they had opted not to talk politics on that occasion—was unable to come to her aid. If help did not arrive soon, she would perish. Absolute freedom or absolute tyranny: that was the watchword passed along to her by Forster, which had enticed her to come to Mainz. That had not changed. Meanwhile, the troops of the Holy Roman Empire were firing down on the city without cease.

Revolutionary wars had been raging in Europe since the previous year, and the French were omnipresent. Austria, Prussia, and allied small states mobilized to fight off the "freedom flu" rampant in France, spreading every which way like a deadly virus. The revolution had advanced to Mainz. It was vitally important for the German rulers to intervene before it was too late.

Sensing the danger that lay ahead, the establishment in the Holy Roman Empire reacted frantically to the political events in Mainz. When the archbishop of Mainz, Friedrich Karl Joseph von Erthal, had to flee his own city, he hastily scratched out the coat of arms displayed on the door of his coach—a ruler by God's grace, he was hounded out of the court by the people's fury. His former personal physician, reasoning that it was better to be safe than sorry, went over to the side of the revolutionaries.

In late May 1793, Carl August, the Duke of Saxe-Weimar, and his minister, Goethe, had joined up with the allied troops. Prussian and Austrian armies now besieged the city, as well as Saxon, Hessian, and Palatinate Bavarian units under the supreme command of the Prussian general Friedrich Adolf von Kalckreuth. The French army was well situated strategically.

Goethe accompanied his duke into war, as he had on the military campaign the previous fall. During that campaign, the armies of the Holy Roman Empire had been forced to admit defeat, which could not happen again. Right up until the decisive strike against the Republic, Goethe spent his time studying the theory of colors, an undertaking he'd had to interrupt for the campaign. Nature, unlike history, is patient. No one can know what lies ahead, what sorts of events will befall a given individual's life. History can progress in leaps and bounds, but the observation of nature shows us that nature does not make such leaps, even though it constantly shifts, even though no formation is identical to any other. Goethe's work contrasted the

Richard Earlom, *The Plundering of the King's Cellar, Paris, August 10, 1793*, mezzotint after a painting by Johann Josef Zoffany, 1795 (detail)

eventfulness of history with the steadiness of nature—an act of self-affirmation in the midst of an era that seemed to be unraveling every which way.

The duke lent him a hand at every turn, welcoming this opportune distraction. Carl August, who, like so many other observers, had initially welcomed the revolutionary events in Paris—he wished to become an "eyewitness"—feared that the demonic spirit of the revolution would at any moment make its way to Germany and ravage whole regions. Mainz was not so very far away from Weimar. If Austria, Prussia, and Russia had not taken a firm stand against the progression of history, riots would likely have broken out already in several regions of Germany. The major powers mounted a malicious campaign to counter the anarchy, but the dire situation only grew worse.

Back in the duchy of Saxe-Weimar, too, the reins were being tightened yet again to ensure that nothing disturbed the peace. Just one year earlier, in 1792, the jurist Gottlieb Heinrich Hufeland wanted to give a lecture about the French constitution, which had recently been ratified by the National Assembly in Paris, but Christian Gottlob Voigt, the executive officer in Weimar, intervened. Not wanting to fall out of favor with the government, Hufeland agreed not to hold the lecture. But Carl August knew that not all scholars in Jena and Weimar were as tractable. He trusted only his closest friends.

In this volatile period, Goethe was once again a step ahead of his duke. When it came time to identify a successor for Carl Leopold Reinhold, a confirmed Kantian and the first occupant of the chair on critical philosophy at Jena, he had already put out feelers to Fichte, who was well known to be an inveterate democrat, and whose reputation as a sympathizer of the revolution had preceded him.

Appointing Fichte as the new intellectual vanguard in Jena made sense for purely professional reasons. He would be an incomparable asset to the university, a magnet for students from all over Europe. He had recently caused quite a stir, in Weimar and beyond, with a tract titled *Reclamation of the Freedom of Thought from the Princes of Europe, Who Have Hitherto Repressed It*. The poet and writer Christoph Martin Wieland, who was responsible for bringing Goethe to Weimar, had spoken effusively about Fichte. But to the anonymous author of a review in the *Allgemeine Literatur-Zeitung*, Fichte was "quite a wretched fellow." At the time, it was hard to imagine a clearer declaration of belief in the ideas of the French Revolution than Fichte's. And Goethe was actually trying to get this "German Jacobin" to Jena? Inconceivable.

There was a great deal of talk about such matters in the field camp outside Mainz as the summer set in on the hills overlooking the Rhine. The allied troops camped between shredded vines, on trampled, mowed-down fields—the farmers had been ordered to scythe them to prevent the French soldiers from sneaking up in the stalks of grain—and awaited the latest dreadful news about the wounded and the dead, which flowed in daily, hourly, without any prospect of changes. The days were hot and dusty, the nights a blissful respite. There was a growing sense of unease in the regiments; time was crawling. Not even with eyes closed could one picture butterflies fluttering over flowers fragrant with honey.

On June 18, 1793, the bombardment began, with shooting night and day. Churches, towers, entire streets were ablaze. On July 23, a good four months after the Republic of Mainz was founded, Austria, Prussia, and allies finally took back the city. Forster's fear that the Germans—these coarse, poor, ignorant people—were incapable of any revolution had been confirmed right down the line. As Goethe and the duke rode through the bombed-out streets, thin threads of smoke drifted across the roofs.

Caroline's release took a circuitous route. In the end, she was transferred to Kronberg, a small town an hour from Königstein and two hours from Frankfurt, where she could go out into the fresh air whenever she liked but where she remained a prisoner. Her youngest brother, Philipp Michaelis, was eventually able to get her out with the help of a close friend who had connections to the Prussian king. She was finally free.

Her reputation besmirched and her body ailing, Caroline entrusted herself to Wilhelm Schlegel, who knew of her plight. As a student in Göttingen, Wilhelm had tried to court this daughter of an esteemed family; back then—when his affection for her was strongest—she had rejected, ignored, and deeply offended him. Now he was seizing this second chance.

Wilhelm traveled straight from Holland to Frankfurt. Caroline was given back her luggage, which had been confiscated at her arrest, but her money was withheld. She stood before him empty-handed, and Wilhelm gave this ostracized and fallen woman his name. The son she had brought into the world in Lucka, a small town in Saxony, while suffering unbearable pain, was left behind with foster parents. Wilhelm Julius would not live past the age of one and a half.

Shortly after marrying in the summer of 1796, Caroline and Wilhelm moved to Jena, at the express invitation of Schiller, who wanted to win over Wilhelm as a friend and as a contributor to his literary journal, *Die Horen*. Life seemed once again to proceed in a calm and steady manner. At first the Schlegels lived at the marketplace in a house belonging to a merchant named Beyer; later they rented a little house with a garden just outside the city. Although Wilhelm had promised Caroline white curtains, gray rags covered the windows, and the house was dingy and small, but it was good enough for the time being. A little while earlier, Wilhelm had translated that beautiful passage from *Romeo and Juliet*: "For stony limits cannot hold love out, / And what love can do that dares love attempt." A kingdom for a balcony!

In the fall they moved to rear-courtyard housing on Leutragasse, one of the prime addresses in the city. It was part of the Döderlein House, where Friedrich Niethammer, the Swabian theologian and philosopher, had been living since 1797. His wife, Rosine Eleonore Döderlein, was the widow of Johann Christoph Döderlein, a church council member who died in Jena in 1792. A portal with a rounded arch separated the front building from the rear courtyard, shielding it from students, who made a gleeful habit of smashing their professors' windows at any sign of unrest. (Jena had known plenty of turmoil even before the revolution in France.) In letting the Schlegels live with him, Niethammer was doing them a sizable favor.

As was typical for faculty housing, this complex was richly appointed, with a library and its own auditorium, with seating for up to a hundred students. Wilhelm hoped he could one day give lectures there on aesthetics and the history of classical literature, his areas of specialization. Preliminary arrangements were already under way. To get to his lecture hall, he had only to walk through the inner courtyard and up a winding staircase.

With Wilhelm at her side, Caroline felt that she was understood and appreciated, and that she was in the right place, for the first time in her life. She found herself growing fond of the tranquil valley in which they now lived. So they would settle down in Jena. She was indifferent to the gossip on the street about her life and her circumstances. If her husband's brother, Fritz, and Fritz's lover, Dorothea, were to move in with them the following year, their communal living arrangement would become even more appealing and dynamic.

Memories of her trying time at Königstein seemed to be fading. But she could not forget that the French Revolution, which spread like wildfire, had revealed its ugly side to her. The revolution had amounted to nothing but a failed utopia—until Schelling arrived in Jena.

Best Regards,
Your Outside World

FICHTE, SCHELLING, AND THE *I*

His appearance was commanding as he stood at the lectern: his head thrown back, those wide cheekbones, that high forehead, the genteel placement of his hands. Just like Schiller nearly a decade earlier, Schelling was poised to speak at the Griesbach Auditorium.

On October 18, 1798, Schelling gave his first lecture in Jena—in fact, the first he had ever held. The students, packed in tightly, were attentive. Schelling was said to be a genius, but he was also considered obstinate and arrogant.

In the course guide, Schelling announced the two series he was offering: public lectures titled "The Concept and Essence of the Philosophy of Nature" and private lectures titled "The System of the Philosophy of Nature Itself According to My Outline."

Schelling described nature as an ever-generating, ever-renewing force that never stands still. For him, just as absolutely everything else could be grasped by way of the idea of the intellect, nature itself was originally one with the intellect. One needed only to adopt the standpoint of reason in order to understand the world as a totality, and to perceive every individual thing with an eye to its inherent unity with all else. He called this "intellectual intuition," in accordance with, yet in opposition to, Kant. This was knowledge in one fell swoop. There was no more talk of the *not-I* that Fichte had sought to derive from an *original I* by means of a strict deductive method. Schelling could not make sense of a reality devoid of sound, shape, and color. All this thinking was directed against Fichte, for whom nature was dead, a mere object on the path to knowledge rather than a thing in itself.

Schelling preached the ancient theory of *hen kai pan* (one and all), Heraclitus's doctrine that everything comes from a single source and everything returns to one. This doctrine dominated the lecture from the first to the last word. It was high time to dispense with tiresome dualities—of concept versus intuition, forms of reasoning versus objects in time and space—which far predated critical philosophy, and essentially went all the way back to Descartes, the founding father of modern philosophy. The intellectual renewal of the era could succeed only if one could look past all the discrete bits and pieces and focus on the infinitely higher unity, superior to everything else.

If Kant's unfinished revolution was ever to be brought to a conclusion, or if the societal antagonism generated by the increasingly evident failure of the revolution in Paris was to be surmounted, the only way forward was by means of a philosophy that drew no distinction between within and without, subject and object, with one single absolute manifest in all forms of reality. Nature, in Schelling's thought, functioned as a medium for the mind to recognize itself and take shape; in the human mind, nature opens up our eyes and provides us the knowledge that it is there. Nature is only another facet of the mind, not a pernicious foreign object.

An idea was taking shape as they sat at the big round table in the tavern and lifted their beer steins, lids clattering, thick smoke rising up from their long pipes. The fraternity brothers were at their favorite gathering spot.

This was not the first time the idea had been tried out. There were not many avenues for the students to vent their displeasure. After heated arguments with the "chocolatists," they had already moved out of the city to protest the relocation of the ducal troops to Jena. Chocolatists were students who thought all disputes could be settled over a cup of hot chocolate; they had no sense of honor, would rather wield the pen than the sword, and reported any illicit duels to the authorities. The presence of the ducal troops was all the incentive that was needed to inspire a defense of academic freedom. These students would have pushed on all the way to Erfurt if the duke had not relented and ordered the military back out of the city, but they did make it as far as Nohra, near Weimar. *Hurrah for academic freedom!*

At some late hour, the time for action had come. The final round of drinks downed, the last guests emerged from the Tanne, as a few others staggered out of the adjacent Geleitshaus, where carters and merchants had to pay the bridge toll. They made their way to the other side of the Saale River. In the middle of the bridge was the stone cross marking the boundary that separated Jena from Camsdorf, and down below, the water moved languidly along. This bridge was the stuff of legends. In the early part of the century, a horse was said to have bolted, jumped over the railing, and carried its rider to his death; on nights when the moon was full, it was said that you could hear the pounding of hoofbeats mingling with the roar of the river.

The city wall out front, the mountains behind. A view up to Jenzig Mountain, the peak of which almost touched the moon at this time of night. Through the city gates, across the Graben. And there it was, the professor's house, right next to the Red Tower. He wanted to ban fraternities, put a stop to obligatory dueling. Would they disband voluntarily? Inconceivable for them. He was another one of those chocolatists.

It was intended as nothing more than a scare tactic. Slinking around the building, shadows—longer, then shorter—cast on the walls. Breathe out, breathe in. Reach back—hold on, there's light in the windows! It just went on. Quick, get to the wall. The stone—from the bank of the Saale, polished smooth by the horses' hooves—is nice and heavy. Murmuring. The light is off. And again: Breathe out, breathe in, then reach back.

A loud crash, and the window cracked. Before anyone in the house had time to react, they ran off, though they would have enjoyed seeing him in a frenzy. Yes indeed: the *absolute I* could certainly fly into a rage as it realized how very alive this *not-I* could be. The hard reality was that the *not-I* could smash windows and be insubordinate and unrelenting; it was not just some ball that the *I* might throw at the wall before catching it in the act of reflection. *Best regards, Your Outside World.*

In the middle of the summer of 1798, when Schelling was working as a tutor in Leipzig, he received a letter from Jena with the privy councilor Johann Wolfgang Goethe's personal signature. Schelling read, stopped short, then went on reading: "You are hereby receiving a copy of the most auspicious decree, which the Serene Highness has issued to the academy in Jena on your behalf." There it was, finally, the long-awaited letter of appointment! Schelling held the decree with the ducal seal in his hands. He hadn't needed to ask for any favors. He was not wanted in Tübingen, where he had attended university, and the tedium there would have been unbearable anyway, as would have been all the tumult, the orthodox reaction to the great Kantian revolution. Back in 1795, he had pulled up stakes, along with his friends and fellow students Georg Wilhelm Friedrich Hegel and Friedrich Hölderlin.

Things were different in Jena: The duke loved the sciences, which was why, early on, he had selected Goethe to serve as a minister at his court, as someone with whom he could share this passion. And Goethe participated in one capacity or another in all important university appointment decisions, as he had in this instance.

Goethe was impressed by Schelling's "On the World Soul," which he had read earlier that year. The idea of the "world soul" sounded like the long-sought magic formula that could encompass all of material nature, of history, of the entire cosmos, and hence bridge the divide that had split apart the era so definitively.

Goethe sought to establish communication with Schelling for the express purpose of learning what could still be expected of philosophy, a field he had often struggled with for being too speculative, far too abstract. He was put off by most of the philosophical literature of his era, so, as he saw it, a philosopher of nature like Schelling had come along at just the right time. After all, Goethe was deeply devoted to natural science, particularly his theory of colors, at times even more than to his own writing. Goethe always saw nature as an element of the mind, the mind always an element of nature—these were not opposites, at least not in the sense that they could not merge in a higher totality. Goethe's discovery of the intermaxillary bone, which had always been taken to be the distinguishing feature between humans and animals, proved that beyond a shadow of a doubt. Man, with his intellect, was not separate from the animals, but developed from the realm of nature. The ancient Aristotelian notion of a *scala naturae*, a Great Chain of Being, an incremental structure of the world, was true as long as one allowed for the possibility that its components could change and need not adhere to a strict predetermined hierarchy. The links in the chain led up from the inorganic to the organic, from the smallest to the largest.

As he read Schelling's theses, Goethe felt a shock of recognition. His contemporaries liked to call him the thinker of the poets, and he now seemed to be standing face-to-face with his own counterpart, the poet of the thinkers. He had been waiting for someone like this.

On Whitsunday, Goethe finally arranged for a three-way meeting with Schelling and Schiller at the latter's garden house. They sat together at the large stone table outdoors under the pergola until the sun went down. Schelling was impressive; he passed the test, and any last reservations were dispelled. Fichte was also supportive, and hoped to meet Schelling that summer in Dresden. Goethe, Schiller, and Fichte were committed to doing all they could to get Schelling to Jena. Schelling could not have wished for better advocacy, particularly because he had not completed a postdoctoral degree—his candidacy conflicted with standard academic norms, which were accorded great importance at the University of Jena. The university did not even compile the usual letters of recommendation.

On July 5, the letter of appointment went out to Schelling. He would begin as an unsalaried associate professor, then would begin offering a private and a public lecture series each semester. Even though he was required to offer the public lectures free of charge, Schelling was entitled to charge a fee for the private ones. He would bring in additional money by circulating weekly course materials to his students. The only thing left to do was to explain to his disappointed parents that he would not be returning to his Swabian hometown anytime soon. But anyone with the opportunity to be a university lecturer in Jena could only, as he put it, "piss on the philosophical wall" back home.

The day that Schelling received the letter of appointment, he resigned from his post as tutor for the Riedesel family. His two young charges would have to get by without him. Dresden was calling—Goethe had told him how highly he thought of the antiquities collections and the gallery at the Neumarkt. In Goethe's view, a concept had to derive from intuition—not the other way around; in speaking about art, one needed to be concrete.

As he prepared for the time ahead in Jena, Schelling stayed in Dresden for a full month and a half. Fritz and Wilhelm, Novalis and Fichte could hardly wait to visit him there.

From a rhetorical standpoint, the first lecture was a catastrophe. Perhaps he needed to talk more slowly, or be better prepared. So far everything had come across as overwrought.

While preparing his presentations, he often found his thoughts turning to Caroline and her ready wit. Just recently, at the reopening of the Hoftheater, they had gotten amazingly close once again. Schiller was being performed, *Wallenstein's Camp*. Images ran through his mind of the new hall, the opening-night postshow festivities, and the ride home, without Wilhelm.

Schelling tried to strike a lofty tone. He was bent on going well beyond the limits of the conceivable, and showed little consideration for those who would not at least try to follow him there. He spoke quickly, far too quickly, rushing along, essentially talking only to himself, barely leaving any time for the ideas tumbling over his lips to unfold and take shape.

Fichte was a true virtuoso at the lectern, known for challenging his students to think independently—and to follow lines of argumentation—in the finest educational tradition, and his expectations were often far too high. An old hand on the lecture circuit, he continually sought direct contact with his audiences. By contrast, Schelling, a newcomer to this mode of address, lacked not only the requisite rhetorical brilliance but also, more pressingly, a sense of openness in engaging with his audience. Fichte was not an eloquent speaker, but his words were clear, and they carried weight. "Think of the wall," Fichte called out to his audience. "Have you thought of the wall? Now, gentlemen, think of the one who thought of the wall"—thus utterly bewildering the audience, because, of course, the act of making oneself the object of reflection can only *itself* bring about an act of reflection in turn, and so on, ad infinitum. One's own *I* cannot be the object of cognition; it is not objectifiable, and can be pinpointed only in an intellectual intuition of something that perpetually precedes experience. *I* is, in actuality, the transcendental subject. The first speculative step toward transcendental idealism had been taken.

Schelling's somber, cryptic lectures had none of this impulsivity. There was no question about it: He had something important to say. But it was difficult even to take notes at his speed. All the same, the audience hung on his every word.

One audience member in particular was quite taken with him. Henrik Steffens, a Norwegian lecturer not much older than Schelling himself, was so fascinated by the idea of a philosophy of nature that he traveled the hundreds of miles from Kiel for the express purpose of attending Schelling's lectures. The evening of the inaugural lecture, he paid a formal visit to Schelling—who had thus landed his first disciple at his very first lesson.

After just a few hours it was evident that the students idolized Schelling as well. They may have understood no more than a fraction of what he had to say, but that was exactly what attracted them, what made him seem inimitable. A perpetual pulling away of things that ought to come together, a magic circle out of which everything arose and into which everything returned. Let the world outside fall to ruins, let Bonaparte triumph or lose, let Europe kneel down before him or join forces against him—Schelling's philosophy, which was a philosophy of the absolute, brought a gleam to everything, making the world grow ever brighter until nothing more could be seen and everything had become clearest light.

The cause of the throngs that appeared near the Stadtschloss during the late afternoon, with crowds forming in front of the Griesbach Auditorium, would soon be apparent to all. Anyone from Jena would know that the hour had struck for Schelling to lecture on the philosophy of nature.

Much Ado

The production was a quite a feat. Goethe himself had lent a hand; he was on the scene from morning till night. He sensed the excitement building up before the premiere of *Wallenstein's Camp.* It would mark the beginning of a whole new era in theater.

Goethe saw that the moment was propitious. The idea of remodeling the Weimar Hoftheater had been under discussion for quite some time, but there was no decisive impetus to move ahead with the project. The opportunity finally arose when the Stuttgart architect Nicolaus Friedrich Thouret came to Weimar to reconstruct the Stadtschloss, the residence of the sovereign Duke of Saxe-Weimar. The presence of a master builder stirred the desire to build.

After 1791—the year the Society of Actors at the Ducal Court was established—it was clear that the old Komödienhaus was no longer adequate to meet the needs of a professional theater troupe. A new hall was needed, a space that provided all audience members a good view of the stage and fine acoustics, which posed both a technical and an aesthetic challenge.

Thouret was equal to both. In a very short time, pillars, galleries, balconies, and curtains had been constructed, and all sorts of items were decorated, painted, and gilded. The renovation work, which began in July 1798, lasted barely three months. By mid-August the interior framework of the theater was in place. The design suggested a Greek theater. Pillars painted to resemble granite formed a semicircle around the orchestra section, which was surrounded on the first tier by eighteen fluted Doric-style columns of Cipollino marble, sometimes referred to as onion stone, below the rising semicircle of the rows of seats. Ultimately, the floor was lowered to accommodate all the planned tiers, to make the space appear less cramped. *Et voilà*—in late September the renovations were complete. Thouret had kept the promise he made to his client. The redesign looked solemn but not oppressive, opulent but uncluttered. There would be three performances a week, on Mondays, Wednesdays, and Saturdays. An exception was made for the reopening: the premiere was scheduled for a Friday.

Goethe was preoccupied with still other matters. He had made changes to the prologue of the new play—nothing major, but still. He could only hope that Schiller wouldn't mind the modifications.

The public was impressed by the new hall, which no longer bore any traces of the baroque "society of patrons" theater of yore. Thouret's design had clean lines, and he was sparing with the use of decorative touches. Only the duke's loge was given distinctive decor; the rest was kept simple. The space looked well structured, and every detail had been carefully thought out. Nothing needed to be subtracted or added. It was the very definition of classicism.

Everyone who was anyone had come to the reopening. The

renowned Weimar fashion magazine *Journal des Luxus und der Moden* sent Karl August Böttiger to cover the story. Böttiger was the ultimate busybody; Schiller called him Magister Ubique (Master Here-There-and-Everywhere), and Schelling even referred to him as a "blowfly" who landed on every group involved with literature and the theater. People had learned to be wary of Böttiger's talent for replicating every word of a conversation in his literary works. Rumor had it that a book about the Weimar circle was already in preparation. Böttiger was a true Weimaraner, sniffing around for information like a bloodhound. His network extended to the French emigrant circles in Weimar. In 1791, on the recommendation of Johann Gottfried Herder, he was appointed director of the secondary school and the chief consistorial councilor for educational affairs.

The stage of the Hoftheater had the same prestige as the pulpit in Saint Peter und Paul, the city church where Herder gave sermons in his capacity as general superintendent. This stage, too, was an institution that focused on morality, the difference being that here morality was not preached, but rather subjected to critical scrutiny. And while Herder had to wait at his pulpit until the room was quiet and the last cough had faded away, the audience at the Hoftheater did not need to be asked to settle down. There was absolute silence from the start.

Theatergoers in Weimar were known for their urbanity; they would not bow to fashion trends or cling anxiously to tradition. The conditions were thus ideal for taking risks and putting the era to the test, which bolstered Goethe's belief that, with Schiller's arrival, Weimar would finally meet the dramatist it deserved.

Schelling, Caroline, and Wilhelm accepted Goethe's invitation and made a special trip from Jena. That summer, Wilhelm had also been appointed to the university as an associate professor, sub rosa, behind closed doors. Wilhelm's ambition was sparked by picturing himself soon at the side of Fichte and Schelling, mounting the highest philosophical echelons, transforming aesthetics and physics into "song," as his brother, Fritz, envisioned. One thing did bother him about the new constellation: Schelling was often a guest in their home, a bit *too* often for Wilhelm's taste. Back in Dresden, the three of them had thought of having Schelling move in with Wilhelm and Caroline; there was certainly ample room. Now they didn't even know who should sit where at the table, so Caroline wound up wedged between the two men.

Before the long-awaited highlight could begin, August von Kotzebue's *The Corsicans* was performed to lead off the evening. Kotzebue had burst with pride when Goethe told him that his play would be presented at the opening—in his hometown! He pictured himself posing with a laurel wreath. But no one had come to see *his* play; something entirely different was on the program that evening. The audience looked around the room impatiently when the introductory offering was finally over, but their curiosity could not rip the curtain apart.

Then it was time for "Poetry" to literally rise to the sky— Thouret had painted this allegorical figure right onto the theater curtain. Just after the curtain rose, Johann Heinrich Vohs, an actor at the court in Weimar, playing the younger version of the protagonist Piccolomini, began to recite the prologue in a sonorous voice; then the first bars of the prelude sounded and the final trumpet blares faded away, followed by soldiers' cheers at the encampment near Pilsen, above which imperial flags and banners nodded down in wild disarray, with a spacious sutler tent and a couple of smaller junk stands in one spot, and a kettle over the fire, around which Croatians and Capuchin monks were gathered. As the play began, Schelling and Caroline, sitting next to each other among all the other invited guests, found their thoughts wandering in entirely different directions.

There was a brief moment of silence when the curtain fell, even before the chorus had finished singing. The audience paused—then burst into thunderous applause. Schiller, who had arrived in Weimar the previous day to have a look at the final rehearsals, was leaning on the balcony railing. Goethe was showered with applause as well. All agreed that the ensemble had put in a fine performance. Everything had come together to form a perfect whole.

After the performance, small groups gathered in the lobby. Glasses clinked, and all the stops were pulled. Rehearsals for *The Piccolomini*, the second part of the *Wallenstein* trilogy, would start in December. The three parts recounted the fate of an important Bohemian general, telling the story of a conflict that pitted submissiveness against self-determination, imperial power against resistance, constraints from without against freedom from within. Gathered in the lobby, audience members recapitulated in their minds and aloud what they recalled about the period of the Thirty Years' War, retelling stories from their family history. They saw their own present eerily reflected in the past, and realized that the "old solid form," the hard-won Peace of Westphalia, had increasingly fallen apart in the wake of the current political events—in Paris, in Rome—and was now basically gone. Would peace ever again be possible in Europe? And what price would people be willing to pay for it? The writer's fantasy had given a voice to history, conjuring up dark times yet looking to more promising horizons. The traces of the past were still right there. The future was open—and had yet to be written.

Fichte was the only one to act undignified after the performance. He was constantly urging the others to drink more

Pieter Snayers, *The Battle of White Mountain*, 1620 (detail)

champagne, topping off their drinks again and again. Caroline felt the effects of his misbehavior more than anyone else, particularly because he must have refilled her glass four times. Schelling had to free her from Fichte's embrace. Fichte was not known as an extrovert, but he was losing his self-discipline—just as critical philosophy can become oblivious when it attempts to adjust reality to align with its categories. When Fichte glanced around, he saw that he was alone.

The man of the evening, the author himself, seemed tense as he left the building. He did not want to let on what he was thinking. In spite of the success of the event, he felt betrayed by Goethe's rather substantial revisions to his prologue. Twelve lines had been taken out and two new ones added; there were quite a few other modifications that could not be passed off as mere cosmetic changes for the audience and the stage, as Goethe had described them beforehand in a letter and again at the dress rehearsal just the day before. Schiller had continued to polish his prologue down to the wire, and had not sent the final version to Weimar until the previous week.

The prologue was essentially the key to the entire work of historical drama that Schiller had in mind. Where might one situate the present, Schiller wondered, in an era that had come apart? But Goethe stripped the prologue of its most radical formulations. In Schiller's version, he had a "new era . . . begin today" on the stage, but in Goethe's, the era merely "appears" as an "epoch" sent by higher powers, a gift from on high. For the published text, Schiller would return to his own—the original. He had no intention of leaving things up to Goethe; the written version would be the final word. As Schiller crossed the square in front of the theater, he was seized by a familiar feeling: that they would have to agree to disagree.

At some point Wilhelm said good night to Caroline; he intended to stay in Weimar and speak to Goethe the following day about the *Athenaeum*, the new literary magazine he had just founded with Fritz. Schelling would get into the carriage with Caroline and travel back to Jena that night. Since the summer, when they had stood together in the picture gallery in Dresden in front of Raphael's *Sistine Madonna*—that meaningful glance, that brief touch—Caroline had felt drawn to the man she considered, as she'd told Fritz in private, "true granite." With him, she could break through walls, the walls that had once held her prisoner in Mainz.

The Dresden Pause
for Artistic Effect

IN THE ARMS OF THE MADONNA

Just a month after he got back to Berlin from Dresden that summer,
Fritz had received a thick envelope from Jena. When he opened
it, he saw right away that inside was "The Paintings," the di-
alogue that Wilhelm and Caroline had begun during the time
they all spent together in Dresden: descriptions and dialogues of
art that gave literary form to their freewheeling conversations.

"The Paintings" read beautifully. He spent two evenings in
a row studying the manuscript. The texts were woven together
cleverly, and constantly switched back and forth between interior and exterior facets that shaped and brought out what had
been seen. Nothing stood in the way of the publication they were
planning for the *Athenaeum*. The journal compiled essays, letters, conversations, rhapsodic meditations, and aphoristic fragments. Fritz was principally responsible for the philosophical
portions, Wilhelm for the contributions on translation and criticism. The magazine was a declaration of war on time-honored
traditions: "Truth" could never be expressed in a halfway manner out of consideration for others. Vapid unanimity would be

unacceptable. Diversity of opinions and perspectives, and conflict, would not merely be tolerated; Fritz and Wilhelm were
explicitly provoking disputes as their declared editorial principle. No one in the group—not Goethe, not Schiller—had ever
been this dedicated to freedom of thought and freedom of the
word. The political revolution in Paris may have failed, but here,
a different one—an aesthetic revolution—was drawing near.

The journal was the ideal placement for a piece of writing
like "The Paintings." The first issue had been published in the
spring, and the next one would soon follow. And while Fritz
read the piece once again, he pictured himself back at the gallery,
on a spirited stroll with the group.

Fritz and Wilhelm had often dreamed of exploring the Dresden
collections. The eminent art historian Johann Joachim Winckelmann had claimed that anyone seeking the sources of art had
to travel to Dresden. The treasures of so many centuries were
openly displayed for study in the antiquities gallery near the Elbe
River, in the refurbished Japanese Palace, in the picture collection
at the Neumarkt section of the inner city, and in the converted
ducal stables just across from the residential palace. Dresden had
developed into the European center of the arts, and had come to
be known as "Athens for artists"—Saxony and Attica, juxtaposed.

The arrival of Schelling, Novalis, and Fichte introduced a
new vibrancy into the group. The Dresden art lovers made their
way through the antiquities collection by torchlight in the evenings, and came early in the mornings to view the picture gallery
in a casual, disjointed sequence, taking notes, pontificating, and
moving on.

Schelling traveled in from Leipzig. In his view, Dresden's

offerings were on a par with those of Rome's Capitoline Museum, the Vatican art collection (including its papal antiquities collection), and the Florentine collection in the Uffizi Galleries.

People were hearing that he had just been appointed to the faculty at the University of Jena. He was young—only twenty-three—and already a rising star in German philosophical circles. There was enormous curiosity about this young man, from whom great things were expected.

Schelling announced that he would remain for several weeks. Dresden was still a relic of antiquity, a place where a bygone world lived on in its statues. It was a shame, though, that the restorations were so sloppy. In the reflection of the torches the group used to make its way through the gallery at night, even their untrained eyes could see all the irregularities, and how crudely the restorers had gone about their work, without any sense of anatomical correctness, let alone how to arrange the figures artistically. It would have been better to present the sculptures as torsos, as fragments, just as history had shaped them over the course of centuries.

Novalis had come in for a brief visit from Freiberg, where he had been studying with the famous mineralogist Abraham Gottlob Werner since the latter half of 1797. Fichte, too, had not wanted to pass up the opportunity to pay a visit to Schelling before the winter semester began. They had met the previous year, at the 1797 fall trade show in Leipzig, after Fichte had failed in attempts to see him in Tübingen, where Fichte had once visited the Tübinger Stift theological seminary, and in Jena, at Pentecost. They had always missed each other, but while they were in Dresden, Fichte wanted to get better acquainted with his future colleague. Everyone was eager to meet the prodigy, to take in the collection alongside him.

Caroline was there as well; in fact, she had traveled from

Jena to Dresden before Wilhelm, back in early May, along with Johann Diederich Gries, the translator and poet, and her daughter, Auguste, who was now thirteen. On May 9, the three set out bright and early, full of anticipation about the summer ahead. Caroline wanted to turn her attention back to things of beauty, at long last. The art treasures in Dresden were just the right destination: a feast for the senses, a meal for the mind.

The illustrious group made its way through the Italian wing, stopping in front of the *Sistine Madonna* to examine the painting's placement of the figures, which resulted in a lavish production. They kept changing their distance from the painting and the angles from which they regarded it, and comparing the varying perspectives. These movements worked quite well, because the painting was not hanging on the wall, as it usually did, but was instead placed on an easel so that painting students could copy and study it. And before they knew it, the visitors found themselves engaged in role play right in front of the painting. There were six people in the picture, and six in front of it. They mimed the figures' body language, including the seemingly bored looks on the cherubs' faces. While Wilhelm, as Pope Sixtus II, kneeled and gazed up at Caroline as the Madonna, Schelling unexpectedly captured the facial expression of the Christ Child.

Oops, what was that? A pause, perhaps a bit too long for merely dramatic purposes. There was a penetrating gaze, and a gentle touch. The others noticed it, too—including Wilhelm.

Only Fichte, who had never really warmed up to issues of art and aesthetics, was unimpressed. Gilt frames, polished floors, and pompous ceremony meant nothing to a philosopher who loved to make pronouncements in the form of imperatives. He stood still, staring into the distance, then dragged himself from picture to picture, from one room to the next. He had told Fritz that he would rather count beans than deal with art. The others'

Raphael, *Sistine Madonna*, 1513

enthusiasm left him cold. Novalis had called the Dresden collections a "sleeping chamber of the future world." Sleep-*inducing*, in fact—how right he had been. Fichte took more pleasure in excursions to the picturesque landscape, the countless valleys and rocky glens, and the secluded spots and villages of Saxon Switzerland.

The fictional construct for "The Paintings" was quite simple at first glance: An art lover, Louise, has come to Dresden with a writer, Waller, and a painter, Reinhold, and they visit the gallery together. Louise chats incessantly, while Waller, who is more reserved, focuses his attention on the antiquities, and Reinhold trudges behind glumly. The conversation takes all kinds of twists and turns, and before they know it, they are surrounded by classics of seventeenth-century Dutch landscape painting, debating the capabilities and limitations of art: How does it stand up when compared to nature, a force of colossal originality that never stands still and is endlessly creative?

Waller regards landscape painting as mere imitation, something that can only fall short when compared with the grandeur of nature. Reinhold disagrees; for him, it depends on how the artist joins objects together, discerning their underlying ideas in his mind's eye and learning to see the world in a new and different way. Louise also tries to persuade Waller that what matters is the formative power of genius, and she launches into a description of the landscape as Jacob van Ruisdael portrayed it for the observer in his painting *The Hunt*: a wooded landscape with trees set far apart on a marshy soil, shining clouds half hidden by the treetops, reflection and shadow, beech trees in bright sunlight with dark sections indicating the approach of fall, and a stag hunt enlivening the scene.

Ruisdael was a landscape artist who truly understood what he was painting. In his works of art, the most commonplace things take on a majestic character. He knew how clouds moved, knew why, at a given moment, they changed their shape, expanded and coalesced, and how light was refracted in the leaves of a tree. Louise describes the picture in all its watery clarity, focusing on the objects that prompt our reflection, speaking about it admiringly without glorifying it or overlooking its shortcomings, yet in the end she finds that it all seems a bit artificial and staged.

The group moves on, right along the Elbe River. Fritz, reading, soon discovered that the fictitious gallery report was more multifaceted than he had been led to believe. Louise, Waller, and Reinhold leave the gallery early and continue their conversation outdoors while gazing across the water as it moves languidly along. Not only do they talk about painting, but they find themselves right in the middle of a painting—Bernardo Bellotto's *Dresden from the Right Bank of the Elbe Below the Augustus Bridge.* Down in the water is a reflection of the tower of the Catholic Church of the Royal Court, then the arches of the bridge, and in the background the dome of the Frauenkirche. Louise begins to draw the picture in the air with light strokes, then traces the commentary about Ruisdael, as she sees it in her mind's eye, onto the landscape, using notes she took in the gallery.

In this way, the fictional trio takes a mental stroll through the gallery once more, and the conversation itself turns into a painting—a painting of a painting—created by the polyphony of their dialogical discourse, which shapes, sums up, and for the first time renders visible what they viewed before. Louise, Waller, and Reinhold begin to see the nature around them with the eyes of artists. The landscape does not compete with the picture in the museum, but rather enters into a synthesis with it by means of the power that inheres in aesthetic intuition. Saxon meadows around the Elbe are mentally juxtaposed with idealized forest landscapes, blending together river barges and stag hunt, marshy soil and the Frauenkirche.

"The Paintings" evoked in Fritz visions of the exuberant days the group spent together in Dresden. They had practical evidence that the "symphilosophizing"—the joint creation of ideas in writing—that they strove to achieve actually worked. There was not much more to keep him in Berlin. In Jena, with Wilhelm and Caroline, Schelling and Fichte, he would feel much freer and be far more productive.

He had been sharing an apartment near Oranienburger Tor with the theologian Friedrich Schleiermacher since meeting him at Henriette Herz's salon, where he did most of his socializing; apart from his lover, Dorothea, this salon was his only consolation in this dusty and draining city. Dorothea and the salongoers were sometimes the only ones who could help him endure the distance from his brother and his other friends, whose wisdom he missed.

In Berlin, the predominant philosophy was that of the time-worn Enlightenment, with a partisan clique in which outsiders neither fit nor had much of a desire to do so. Berlin had Friedrich Nicolai; August von Kotzebue; Garlieb Helwig Merkel, who was already making his presence known from Weimar; and many others of that ilk. Fritz's desire grew—to have Wilhelm and Caroline, Schelling, Fichte, and Novalis close by once again, as they had been in Dresden; to leave the cliquishness of Berlin for the expanse of the Thuringian landscape, where "nectar and ambrosia" flowed, as Caroline had described it to him again and again. *In Jene life is bene,* as the students liked to say. It would be ridiculous to let the opportunity slip by. The plan did not come about overnight; Dresden had just been the beginning, and he had been to Jena before. The idea was to establish an intellectual community there—a republic of free spirits.

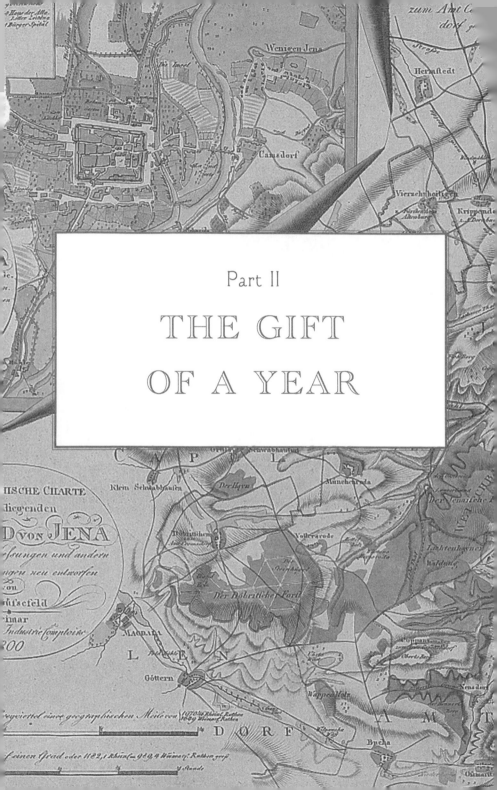

Part II

THE GIFT
OF A YEAR

The Most Beautiful Chaos

LUCINDE, OR THE AUDACITY OF LOVE

When Dorothea finally arrived to meet Fritz in Jena in late 1799, she found her lover in an almost pathological state of melancholy. His worries about the progress of his work were eating him up. Sometimes he sat there, barely responsive, propping up his head with his elbows, his thumb and index finger drawing slow circles toward each other down from his forehead, then between his eyes to the tip of his nose. At some point he would glance at whatever English-language book Wilhelm was translating at the moment, usually Shakespeare; *Henry IV* lay on the desk just then. A few moments later his fixed gaze would reveal that once again he had been unable to get himself to write. He'd return to propping up his head and rubbing his temples in a constant circling motion before he flopped down on the sofa in exhaustion. Dark thoughts, troubled sleep. There was nothing Dorothea could do.

The trip to Jena had been sheer torture. Fritz had headed off from Berlin in early September, but she had stayed behind for a few more weeks in order to see to custody arrangements for Philipp, her son from her first marriage. By the time she set out on the journey, the streets were almost impassable. Several times the coach got stuck, and the travelers had to get out in the rain so the horses and carriage could move again. At one point the two horses in front sank so deep in the mud that it took hours to free them up, with the aid of farmers who were summoned to help. It went on like this day after day.

Dorothea had often imagined their reunion. As she lay awake through long nights, writing letter after letter to Fritz, she pictured the carriage approaching the city, Jenzig Mountain in the background standing out in sharp relief, next to it the tower of Saint Michael's Church; her mind's eye moved across the placid valley and the city, a grand panorama that she, a city girl from Berlin, found moving yet almost intimidating, both sublime and sweet. Then she envisioned herself traveling across the river, turning onto the street where she would step out of the carriage, hearing one last snort from the horses, and see Fritz coming down the stairs, slowly, as though he were not the least bit eager to hold her in his arms again after not having seen her for so long, and Wilhelm, too, would appear in the doorway with Caroline, the sister-in-law she was eager to win over, and whom she had known only from letters up to this point. This was to be more than a reunion; it would be the moment that knitted the family together. And now, with Fritz's despondency, things had taken an unexpected turn.

Dorothea and Fritz had stood by each other; that was not the problem. Leaving Berlin had been the right thing to do. But Dorothea could tell that something was holding him back, though she could not bring up the subject. Wilhelm finished a poem every morning, and all the others were making progress on their projects. Ludwig Tieck was now writing a drama, *Genoveva*, which he hoped he could soon present to the master, Goethe, and she herself, Dorothea, was working on her new novel, yet Fritz grew gloomier with each passing day. And there was not even any decent wine to be had.

One evening, Fritz was writing in terza rima, and every time he jotted down a verse, he would dash out of his attic room and down into the parlor, a full three flights, two steps at a time, then stand before her breathlessly, as though he'd been stung by a wasp. Dorothea did not know what to make of his behavior. She liked the verses—no doubt about that—but the way he was carrying on . . . Fritz, who was under tremendous pressure, snarled at her that the second part of *Lucinde* had to get done. He would face dire consequences if he proved unable to complete the project he had laid out for himself.

The first part of *Lucinde* had heralded a literary revolution. Just as the concluding portion of Schiller's *Wallenstein* trilogy— *Wallenstein's Death*—was premiering in Weimar in the spring of 1799, staged by Schiller himself and directed by Goethe, Fritz's novel was published, and it was far more fanciful than his contemporaries could have anticipated. Schleiermacher claimed that at any moment the book could disintegrate into its component parts, yet it constantly came together again, "as though from a future world that is God knows how far away."

Many forms converged in this novel: letters, dialogues, aphorisms, diary entries. *Lucinde* burst open literary genres from within, reached for the "most beautiful chaos," and wound up turning into an "aesthetic monstrosity," in the view of some critics—while others hailed the novel, which resisted pigeonholing as such, for its formal and linguistic originality. And while Schiller's Max Piccolomini throws himself into a hopeless battle against the Swedes, which ends up costing him his life, Schlegel's male protagonist, Julius, who is head over heels in love with his female counterpart, takes up the fight for his love, ultimately invoking the motto "Even though this world may not be the best or most useful, I still know that it is the most beautiful," before succumbing to his passion.

Lucinde is about love, a topsy-turvy reenvisioning of time that outmaneuvers attempts to rein in the moral order and leaves morality behind by invoking aesthetic intuition, overcoming even the distance between partners through dreams, fantasies, and imagination. Julius is the lover and writer; Lucinde, the lover and nonconformist. The plot is minimal; the novel revolves solely around the couple's discovery of love as a way of life that subverts traditional patterns, highlighting the eternal duality of devotion and fidelity, friendship and marriage, elation and abstinence.

Gender relations are inverted, and the irreconcilable polarity of man and woman falls away. In Schlegel's view, overblown femininity and exaggerated masculinity were both one-sided, tedious, and backward-looking. The genders ought to complement each other and form one gender, namely, that of the human being; there should be no other. No more male domineering aggressiveness and female selfless devotion. The contrasts needed to be balanced out. Julius's conclusions are as radical as can be: "I can no longer say 'my love' or 'your love'; the two are identical and perfectly united, as much love bestowed as requited."

Caroline was excited as she relayed her first impressions of the novel to Novalis. What could this book be compared to? All of it clashed with conventional notions about marriage, established forms of relationships, decency, and propriety. Love had no use for external structures; it was the form of life itself. Love and morality, commitment and fidelity did not need to be regarded as true opposites, as long as each was regarded in correlation with the other. Caroline thought that the witty novels of the humorist Jean Paul might be raised in comparison, but

Lucinde couldn't be compared to those either—nothing at all could be compared to the work of the singular writer Jean Paul. As Caroline had recently learned in a conversation with Fichte's very prim and proper wife, even he had read the novel three times already, and found that it got better each time.

It was beside the point that Fritz's novel bore autobiographical characteristics, that Fritz was easily recognizable in the character of Julius, and Dorothea—or even Caroline—in the character of Lucinde. Instead of authenticating the written text by comparing it to reality, readers needed to recognize that the writing itself infused reality, thus becoming the reality in need of this infusion.

The consequence of the ingenious game Fritz Schlegel played with his readers was unending bafflement, confronted as they were by one cascade of genitives after another; like a mirror image lost in its own mirror image, the reader's reflection was steered into the depths of the text, and there one came upon a novel that essentially contained itself. That was precisely Schlegel's strategy, because it revealed something essential about reality—that it, too, was rarely as clear-cut as people thought, and it, too, sometimes started to flicker, to oscillate nervously between the extremes.

Backlash from smug, prissy Berlin was inevitable. The novel seemed like a foreign substance invading the fusty decorum of the salons of Berlin. It was received as shameless, "filthy nonsense." Even Schiller stabbed Fritz in the back, panning the book as the "height of modern formlessness and affectation." It had clearly hit a nerve. Only a moribund era, even one that held its critical faculties in such high esteem, would react this way. Fritz had zoomed far ahead of his era, as he himself knew. Perhaps the novel should not have appeared in print at all, or at least not at the time. Fifty years hence, it might have been read as a novel that would make readers wish it had been published fifty years earlier. The vehemence with which reactions came swirling at Fritz proved to him that he was on the right track, yet he could not shake the feeling that he might lose his mind on the quest to complete the second part.

The city may not have been beautiful, but at least Dorothea had arrived. Money was tight, and the gender roles were not on as equal a footing as she had hoped: while Fritz and Wilhelm worked during the day, she ran the household with Caroline, tended to Philipp and Gustel, and took care of the house and the guests. The house also needed a good spring cleaning. She seldom found time for the finer things in life. Caroline took an active role in Wilhelm's Shakespeare translations, reviews, and essays, and Dorothea forged ahead on her first novel, to be called *Arthur*. At least she was receiving monthly financial support from Simon Veit, her ex-husband, but she had come away from her marriage to him with only a small number of possessions— including her piano—and those had been left behind in Berlin. Now she needed to be thrifty.

Veit, the banker she had married in 1783 at the age of eigh-teen, had made for a respectable match. Having bankers in the family had become somewhat of a tradition. Her mother, Fromet, was born into the Guggenheim merchant family of Hamburg; her ancestors included influential Viennese bankers, notably Samuel Oppenheimer, who handled royal finances. Her father, the famous philosopher Moses Mendelssohn, had arranged for the union when she was fourteen years old. The marriage was devoid of heart and spirit. Veit, a dull, calculating, uneducated man, talked only about business. There could be no comparison to the far more quick-witted man, some twenty years younger, with whom she had now decided to share her life. Luckily, Simon and Dorothea were able to come to an agreement: he left their son in her care, and paid alimony. She was granted custody on the condition that she would not turn her back on the Jewish faith.

Dorothea lived happily with Philipp in her new residence at Leutragasse 5 and felt that she was getting smarter and more skillful by the day. She loved that their new home was full of quirky individuals who looked down on the neighbors who avoided them, considering them philistines. She didn't care. No one who was not privy to her new household's inner circle could imagine the plethora of wit and poetry, art and science surrounding her.

Still, there was no lack of friction. Alliances were forged, philosophical concepts torn apart, prickly remarks bandied about. When it came to Caroline, Dorothea held back. She noticed that Wilhelm's wife had been sizing her up from the very first day, no matter how much kindness Caroline displayed openly. Dorothea was short—much shorter and wider than Caroline. When Dorothea looked in the mirror, she often concluded that she was not pretty: her eyes were big, quite reddened, even somehow burning, her face haggard and hardened. Sometimes she wished she had some of the "lordly audacity" with which Caroline—the admirable hostess, art critic, shining light in every way—pulled off their lunch gatherings as though she had been doing it all her life, without a trace of arrogance. Kant, who had recently been the subject of conversation at the lunch table, as he often was, called behavior like theirs "unsocial sociability," by which he meant a kind of natural antagonism that inhered in human coexistence, a chaotic mixture of conflicting interests. Kant explained that on the one hand, man is predisposed to associate with others, "because in these kinds of circumstances he feels he is more than man, that is, more than the development of his natural capacities," but on the other he also strives for isolation, "because he also finds within himself the unsocial characteristic of wanting everything to go solely to his liking." And this was where conflict originated: friction in social interaction, a resistance that, despite a certain element of tragedy, had something altogether positive about it, because it exerted a disciplining, tempering, and cultivating effect. People needed to realize that they needed their fellow men to achieve their goals, even if they strongly disliked those fellow men, for, sooner or later, one's goals would no longer be individual but common. And in this way, Kant concluded dialectically, "the first true steps [are taken] from barbarism to culture."

Dorothea, Caroline, Fritz, and Wilhelm made a pact to call themselves *Symmenschen* ("sym people") as part of a set of coinages to refer to those who were highly adept, jointly and individually, at both *symphilosophieren* (philosophizing as a group) and *symfaulenzen* (idling as a group). And even though Wilhelm still had a restless, rash way about him, of which Fritz felt he needed to be cured, the group collectively embodied a higher unity, which they aimed to fight to maintain in the future. Caroline and Wilhelm, Dorothea and Fritz had no choice but to embrace the opportunity to form this higher unity. It was a good thing that they had decided to reject the idea of sharing a household with Fichte in Berlin that summer. If German literature, which still lagged so far behind other national literatures, were to be moved into the revolutionary mode in which someone like Fritz would like to see it, they would have to effect such a change there, in Jena, together.

The Imagined Subject

FICHTE BEFORE THE LAW

It was torture. Under the heat of the sun, Johann Gottlieb Fichte fought his way through the sandy wastelands of the state of Brandenburg. In that summer of 1799, they were the equal of an Arabian desert in every regard.

His first impression of the capital of the Prussian kingdom was disheartening. Berlin struck him as dusty and dull, particularly in light of the fact that he had just come from Jena, which he would never have opted to leave of his own free will.

Fritz had arranged for him to get a furnished room at Unter den Linden, for a rate not much higher than for comparable lodgings in Jena; it would have been quite tolerable but for the bedbug infestation. They were under the loose wallpaper, in the upholstery, between the bed frame and the mattress. Fichte complained to Fritz and to his landlord, but everyone downplayed the issue, as this same misery was found everywhere in Berlin. If he really did stay on in that city, he would be in urgent need of new, clean accommodations.

At least he found no fault with the servant he hired just after his arrival, an unassuming and hardworking man with good penmanship, which came in handy when Fichte needed

Illustration from Guillaume Antoine Olivier's *Entomologie, ou, Histoire naturelle des insectes*, Paris, 1789–1808

things written and copied. Of primary importance to Fichte at this juncture was to structure his days so that he could continue working. His current writing project would bear the title *The Vocation of Man*.

For Fichte, structure meant getting up at six in the morning and heading straight to his desk. Mornings were reserved for work; grooming—washing up, combing his hair, powdering his face, dressing—could wait until twelve-thirty. At one, he went to Ziegelstrasse, just on the other side of the Spree River, to have lunch, where he often met Dorothea, who lived alone after separating from Veit. Besides Fritz and Fichte, she was usually joined at the table by Friedrich Schleiermacher, Fritz's friend and the chaplain at the nearby Charité hospital.

In recent times there had been a good deal of discussion about Schleiermacher's new book, *On Religion*, to which the short, hunchbacked theologian gave the sharp-tongued subtitle *Speeches to Its Cultured Despisers*. Schleiermacher was well aware that he could hardly expect to be taken seriously by those who were steeped in the wisdom of the century and had no interest in contemplating eternity. They did not care to hear about a heavenly spark that awakened the dead and brought a glow to all that was drab. For Schleiermacher, religion was beholden neither to morality nor to the Church; it entailed envisioning the universe in its totality. Fichte did not quite know what to make of this outlook, but he enjoyed being Schleiermacher's sounding board.

Once he was back at three o'clock, he would read a French novel or whatever else he came across; then, at about five, he would go to the theater to see a comedy, ride out to the Tiergarten, or walk back and forth before the front door, where the linden trees were in full bloom. On occasion he went on excursions to the country with Fritz, Dorothea, and Schleiermacher.

Since Fichte had come to Berlin, he spent time essentially only with Fritz and his circle. Fritz was also the one to give him the all-clear signal: As long as the particulars that had resulted in Fichte's dismissal and departure from Jena were not revealed, he would not be bothered by officials.

The allegation leveled against Fichte in Jena—atheism—was no minor matter. In the presence of the duke, he had threatened to resign if he should be censured and if the freedom of his teachings was to be restricted in any way by this defamatory accusation. It was no sooner said than done: the censure came and, with it, his dismissal. Fichte had gambled away his chance of remaining.

Fritz strongly advised Fichte against applying for a long-term residence permit, and instructed him to state that he was in Berlin merely "for a visit." It needed to look as though Fichte were simply seeking a distraction, a little change of pace from his everyday routine at the university. If the rumor were to arise that he was on the run, he would immediately become the object of local gossip, which would be unbearable. Moreover, Fritz advised him, he should come to the city just a few days before the king's return.

Friedrich Wilhelm III was regarded as reform-minded, perhaps a bit awkward in his interactions with people, but quite the charmer in comparison with Friedrich Wilhelm II, *der dicke Lüderjahn* (the fat good-for-nothing) who had transferred the affairs of state to him two years earlier, when he was practically on his deathbed. Rumor had it that the king and his wife, Luise, née von Mecklenburg-Strelitz, wished to stop in Weimar to see the final part of Schiller's *Wallenstein* trilogy.

Fritz insisted that if it should emerge that the authorities wished to drive Fichte out of the city, the Prussian king himself would have to decide his case. When the freedom of the word was threatened, he declared, freedom of thought was also imperiled. Fichte's case was no isolated incident; it was emblematic of an era that set great store by its enlightened status.

On July 1, Fichte left Jena, without his wife and his son, uncertain of whether he would ever see the city again. Two days later, on the evening of July 3, he arrived in Berlin, alone, just as Fritz had counseled him. It remained to be seen when he would be able to arrange for Johanna and little Immanuel Hermann to join him.

When Fichte came home at night, he usually dined on no more than a milk roll with a glass of Médoc, the only palatable wine on hand. At ten or eleven o'clock he went to bed. These were dreamless nights, except for once, when Fichte dreamed that his ailing young son was healthy again after going in and out of critical condition. Fichte always kept a lock of his son's hair at hand, to remember him by if the worst should come to pass. In the dream, his child was lying peacefully in his arms. All of a sudden, however, he grew pale, expanded, morphed, and assumed bizarre shapes. Memories of his grimaces continued to wrench Fichte out of his thoughts while he sat at his desk and gazed out the window at the blossoming lindens, as though he were being pursued by those contorted expressions.

The instrument of philosophy was the imagination. The residents of the house on Leutragasse were in full accord on this point. Imagination did not signify fiction, illusion, or deception, but rather an integration of the infinite into the finite, so that eternity assumed its place within the framework of time. The imagination had the ability to mediate contrasts, and at that time there were more than enough contrasts to go around.

Kant had already defined this mediating role: The imagination vividly depicted an object, thus obviating the need for the object to be physically present. It evoked an object not actually there, and its double function—the ability to make something absent into something present and to make something present go back to being absent—lent it the ability to convey contradictions.

The philosophical and literary works of Fritz Schlegel, Wilhelm Schlegel, Schelling, and Novalis relied on the power of the imagination, and trusted in its elasticity. They had all attended the same school—Fichte's. He had been the first to elevate the imagination to the rank of a philosophical principle by combining the *I* with the *not-I*, the world.

The imagination need not come down on one side or the other; Fichte invoked the image of hovering to describe its movement between the two. The imagination hovered between the contrasts, engaging in a subtle, barely perceptible flickering between concept and perception, rationality and sensuality, mind and nature, idea and experience.

But even Fichte had not gone far enough in pinning down the imagination. By placing concepts above perception, rationality above sensuality, and mind over nature, he made the world as a whole dissolve into a mere construct on the part of the subject. In his thinking, reality became a screen onto which the *I* had always projected its image of the world. The *I* shaped the world in keeping with its categories, and nature stayed dead. The matter could not be left at that.

The imagination was not merely a function of comprehension, as Kant and Fichte had defined it. It was a form of reality, because reality itself, in its deepest essence, was made up of contradictions. Fritz, Wilhelm, Schelling, and Novalis were in agreement on this point. A mere concept was blind to feelings;

the understanding was unreceptive to questions concerning the ordinary course of life, the mind too abstract for the structures of living, organic nature. More was at stake—existence itself, in all it comprised, with all its contradictions and moments of failure, just like the revolution in France. Without contradictions there would be no life at all—only death.

While Novalis described the imagination as a perpetual oscillation in which consciousness never slept, Schelling likened it to a first awakening. To him, finite human understanding existed on the basis of the difference between what had always been and what was on the cusp of forming. We awaken from a loss of self as if from a state of death, Schelling explained, and see ourselves positioned in time; the first unassailable act of self-awareness has taken place, an act that will forever remain a blind spot in our consciousness. But the modern era, characterized by this irreconcilable difference, offers us the opportunity to exercise our freedom—which may well be the greatest gift the gods have bestowed on us—and hence also sets out the greatest task for us as human beings.

Fichte's career as an academic educator was checkered. Not one of his colleagues was more esteemed in Jena, yet none was the object of more intense hostility. Fichte had convictions, and that made him vulnerable. Just as the French nation had torn people away from the chains imposed from without, his philosophy aimed to enable people to tear away from the chains in themselves, from dogmatism, and to become autonomous beings. His system set out to be the first system of freedom.

By the time he received his letter of appointment for Jena in 1794, the passion with which the students had greeted the revolution in France had evaporated. There was no trace left of the early enthusiasm that Kant had hailed as a "sign of history." Kant had said that the overwhelming reaction of the public—the magazines that sprang up like mushrooms, the opposition to censorship—would never be forgotten. Fichte sought to rekindle this enthusiasm, and to bring the revolution back to the university.

His first lectures focused on the vocation of the scholar. An academic, he argued, may not stand apart from society; his task is instead to acquit himself well within it, as an innovator, proponent of enlightenment, and promoter of progress. Freedom had to be defended not only at the lectern but also in practice. Ideas needed to be translated into action. The university could not continue to be a mere institution of knowledge, a secluded island cut off from the rest of society; it should—and must—become an active participant. Theory and practice were one and the same. Fichte's philosophy of freedom was a philosophy of action in the truest sense. That was the first essential point to grasp about his idealism.

The spark ignited: The Griesbach Auditorium, where Schiller had held his inaugural lecture, was soon too small for Fichte as well. The students—more than half the entire student population at Jena—crowded throughout the hall and even spilled out into the courtyard. The students soon referred to him as the "Bonaparte of philosophy." This was no mild-mannered philosophizer; Fichte, a short, broad-shouldered man, looked like a warrior at the lectern, his head in constant motion, as though a thunderstorm were erupting at the front of the classroom. Some claimed that Fichte was not merely argumentative but downright belligerent. Never did a gentle word cross his lips. He was a restless spirit on a relentless quest for opportunities to act. Fichte seemed to have declared war on the world that confronted his philosophical *I*.

Debates on the revolution and the freedom of man now took place beyond the confines of lectures and seminars. At Fichte's instigation, the Literary Society of Free Men, which was founded shortly before his arrival in Jena, finally took shape as well. The society's inaugural session on June 18, 1794, featured a debate on "the dawning freedom of man in society in our era, based on principles of reason." Every two weeks the group gathered at a member's apartment to listen to a speech or to discuss an essay that had been circulated in advance. Niethammer, the theologian, generally joined in as well. The Döderlein House had ample room to host these spirited debates. Heinrich Eberhard Gottlob Paulus, his colleague, also took part. When Johann Smidt, a student from Bremen, gave a talk about the ennobling effect of festivities, the group decided that very evening to indulge in a bacchanalian frenzy every second month. *In vino veritas? In veritate vinum!* A true bond of friendship soon extended beyond the group's academic activities. Two days after the birth of his son, Immanuel Hermann, Fichte made a snap decision to register a member of the circle, Johann Erich von Berger, in the church records as the baby's godfather—without Berger's knowledge.

Fichte even instituted a lunchtime gathering, though it did not take long for him and his wife, Johanna, to realize that this sort of thing was unheard of in tranquil Jena. As many as ten students, from Saxony, Swabia, Bremen, Oldenburg, Silesia, Courland, Switzerland, Denmark, France, and Scotland, joined the group on any given day, crowding around a single table. The participants openly exchanged views on the latest developments in politics, literature, and art—a daily journal in the form of conversation.

This sort of freewheeling conversation was not to everyone's liking. On one occasion, when a participant advocated the French cause quite openly—a Jacobin cap was passed around, the Marseillaise struck up—a Scottish participant refused to take part, and left the table just as the soup was served. To a supporter of the aristocracy, these lunchtime conversations were not necessarily good for the digestion.

Some of Fichte's colleagues were also put off by his culture of discussion, claiming that his philosophy contained within it a potential for riots, and there was no telling what damage it might do someday. Fichte kept getting embroiled in controversies, such as when he suggested that the secret fraternities voluntarily disband, all in the interest of the students, of course. After all, he argued, what rational people could still wholeheartedly engage in duels?

Fichte's initiative gave rise to fierce student resistance. The dispute reminded people of the confrontation with the chocolatists, the incursion of the ducal troops, the exodus of students as they headed to Erfurt. To teach Fichte a lesson, the students smashed his windows. He and his family fled the city and spent most of the summer of 1795 on an expansive estate in Ossmannstedt, close to Weimar, the former summer residence of the dowager duchess and an oasis of peace and happiness. But the atmosphere in Jena remained highly charged—one little spark, and the powder keg would explode.

That point was reached when Fichte was accused of promoting atheism after the *Philosophisches Journal* published his essay "On the Basis of Our Belief in a Divine Governance of the World" in October 1798. Little in this essay could be deemed atheistic in the strict sense; Fichte was merely taking a stand against an overly simplistic anthropomorphization of God. God could not be thought of as an individual enthroned somewhere

in heaven, wrote Fichte; He could only be the moral world order, and nothing else. To speak of God as an individual, a func-
tioning entity, would mean to deny God's existence.

It took exactly five days for the first notice to arrive from
neighboring Saxony. The Saxon elector, Frederick Augustus III,
called on Duke Carl August in Weimar to withdraw the issue
from circulation, with the claim that the essay was incompatible
with either Christian or natural religion. One could not stand
by idly while, just across the Saxon border, outspoken teachers
were attempting to cast God and religion out of people's hearts,
thus endangering their own students. If there were no change
to the situation in Jena, officials would be forced to prohibit the
university's students from attending.

The allegations of seduction of youth and denial of the deities
were as old as philosophy itself. Fichte suddenly found himself
pressed into the role of Socrates, in whose day, as in Fichte's,
the true triggers were political. For German princes, dukes, and
kings, Fichte was a dangerous author, a political visionary, a
reprehensible democrat, a notorious Jacobin, a ticking bomb.
The notice was essentially a means of lashing out at the entirety
of Kant's critical legacy.

The pressure on the Weimar government grew. More and
more royal courts banned the *Philosophisches Journal* and threatened to pull their young people out of the University of Jena.
For Carl August, the "Causa Fichte" grew more volatile with
each passing day. This sympathizer of the revolution had been
suspect to him from the outset. Just as quickly as he had placed
his trust in Goethe, back when they spoke about the appointment plans in Mainz, he now withdrew it from Fichte. Too
much was at stake for the duke. Even though Fichte himself
soon penned a defense addressing the actual accusations against

him and more than two hundred students signed a petition to retain their beloved teacher, his days in Jena were numbered. No one—not even Goethe—was rushing to help him.

Shortly after Fichte's arrival in Berlin, the police came knocking at his door for a routine visit. The city was divided up into various districts, each presided over by a commissioner who needed to be informed about any new resident. He was asked whether he planned to settle down in Berlin.

As he had arranged with Fritz, Fichte stated that he was there only for pleasure and couldn't say how long he would be staying. They appeared to buy this explanation. But Fichte knew he was now under observation, so he approached his correspondence with caution. Schelling, who was waiting for a message from him, would have to be patient. Fichte opted to convey confidential notes by way of friends, such as Ludwig Tieck.

At this time, people took a careful look at the letters they received before opening them so they could determine whether someone had tampered with them. Incoming mail was best sent directly to Schleiermacher at the Charité hospital, but not to Fritz, whose letters were also being inspected; this was how Fichte and Johanna had stayed in touch during his initial period of exile in Berlin. At the same time, Fichte could not call a total halt to his official correspondence, which would only arouse suspicions and set the administrative hounds on his trail.

The situation was precarious, but Johanna stuck with him through all the uncertainties. He had no support system in Berlin. His connection with Fritz, whose *Lucinde* was considered indecent, rubbed some prominent members of society the wrong way. They could not understand why Fichte would associate with someone like this, particularly because Fritz was living with a woman out of wedlock. Fichte held back from pronouncing judgment on the novel. But to his own surprise, he was quite taken with how it could convey contrasts by means of the imagination. He read *Lucinde* three times, but mentioned this to no one apart from his wife (who told Dorothea).

Fritz and Dorothea decided to go to Jena, but wouldn't it be far better for Wilhelm and Caroline to come join the group in Berlin instead? Fichte actually suggested setting up a kind of communal household for exchanging ideas and living under one roof, and he made the case for this setup to all parties in question. Schelling could join them as well; why not? They could rent a big place in the city, hire a cook, live together like one big family. An academic post would turn up, one way or another. But the others were evidently intent on sticking with their choice. Dorothea had even already made arrangements to rent out the furniture in her apartment. They did not appear to be giving any serious consideration to his suggestion. Fine, he thought—let them figure it out for themselves.

Helping Hands

It was bitterly cold when Goethe returned to Jena with Schiller after the premiere of *The Piccolomini* in February 1799. Snow had fallen, knee-high. A carriage ride seemed out of the question. They opted for the season-appropriate alternative: a sleigh ride.

Like *Wallenstein's Camp*, which had opened the preceding fall, *The Piccolomini* was an all-out success—for the dramatist, Schiller; for the director, Goethe; for the refurbished hall of the Weimar Hoftheater; and for the architect, Thouret. And to top it off, its opening fell on the birthday of Carl August's wife, Grand Ducal Highness Luise, née von Hessen-Darmstadt. After premiering on January 30, the play had to be performed a second time three days later at the express wish of the audience. It was a sensation.

The critics agreed that *The Piccolomini* was one of the best plays to be presented on a German stage in quite some time. You could almost see the audience condensing Schiller's lines into maxims, giving them a life of their own, turning them into quotable sayings: "No hour strikes for the happy man."

Bundled in fur coats and blankets, Goethe and Schiller set off.

Goethe needed distance for now: from the theater and from Weimar, where he was a privy councilor, minister of state, and adviser to the duke. He traveled to Jena as a writer. There he would be able to concentrate better than at the court, where his duties and daily social obligations kept him away from matters he deemed essential. Schiller had already chided him for having taken such a long break from literary texts, and reminded him that this sort of hiatus could not recur. Goethe would have to insist on carving out the time he needed. He already had an idea of what to write next: he would take up where he had left off on *Faust*, his long-term project.

Goethe was not entirely free of obligations in Jena either; as soon as he announced his arrival, he was flooded with requests. Goethe supported causes pertaining to the University of Jena; tended to the scientific institutes and collections, especially in anatomy, the field he was most passionate about; and kept in touch with many scientists. He relished the quiet hours he spent pursuing his studies in the tower of the anatomy building. There, together with Justus Christian Loder, the head of the anatomy department, he had made his great discovery of the human inter-maxillary bone. He had not merely suspected that it existed; he had always *known* it did.

He also had to attend to matters such as the expansion of the road linking Weimar and Jena, which was at the mercy of rainwater and streams. A few years earlier he had followed the news about aerostats, "newfangled hot-air balloons" used to travel in the sky. The Montgolfier brothers had watched their aircraft rise up into the air before the eyes of the king of France. On board were a sheep, a rooster, and a duck, and all survived. Shortly thereafter, animals were followed by humans, who were treated to a bird's-eye view of the whole land. All at once, with

Contemporary depiction of the first flight of a hot-air balloon, on
September 19, 1783, witnessed at Versailles by King Louis XVI,
Queen Marie Antoinette, and Benjamin Franklin

man's newfound ability to sail through the air, the trials and tribulations of earthly things were unfurled and decipherable.

On several occasions, Goethe himself had experimented with building hot-air balloons, together with Wilhelm Heinrich Sebastian Bucholz, the Weimar court pharmacist. The duke personally commissioned the production of a balloon of this kind. Efforts at the dowager duchess Anna Amalia's estate to send up a small balloon made of ox bladders did not get far, which did not deter some of the project's backers from dreaming of a trip into outer space, to the moon and back. (Getting to Jena and back without undue difficulty wouldn't be bad for a start, either.)

Goethe often spent several days in a row in Jena, sometimes even an entire month, far away from his common-law wife, Christiane Vulpius, who had to take care of their son and run the household in his absence. At times it seemed to people in Weimar that Goethe no longer lived in his house on Frauenplan at all; he no longer greeted guests at the dark ebony door bearing the Latin inscription *Salve*.

When Goethe was in Jena, he usually spent the night in a small, simply furnished room on the top floor of the Stadtschloss. Once the duchy of Saxe-Jena had reverted to its Weimar neighbor in 1690—after Jena spent only eighteen years as the royal seat—the premises were used for other purposes. Beginning in 1779, the Stadtschloss housed a library, along with a highly diverse set of collections. Goethe most often consulted the mineralogical collection, which he oversaw with Professor Johann Georg Lenz.

Up there on the top floor, he would enjoy a cup of hot chocolate, which he had loved since Alexander von Humboldt, the worldly-wise natural scientist, had recommended it to him. Humboldt explained that, in the cocoa bean, nature exhibited its most successful condensing of its most valuable nutrients into one small space. Goethe had recently learned that Humboldt was planning to explore the Americas, traveling from La Coruña in northwest Spain to Caracas by way of the Canary Islands, heading from there through the Latin American world. Every time Goethe brought the hot cup to his lips, he could not help but think of Humboldt's words. The chocolate truly hit the spot. Whenever he felt the craving, he even arranged to have the shop Riquet, in Leipzig, send him his favorite brand of chocolate. It was just the right follow-up to an excursion through the snow-covered landscape. As soon he arrived back at the Stadtschloss, freezing cold, he would ask Carl, his servant, for a cup of hot chocolate.

("Carl" was the name he used for all his servants. The long years and close connection he had shared with his original servant made it difficult to adapt to a new name. But while the great Kant, who grew forgetful as he got on in years, consistently misspoke by using the same name for the successor of his longtime servant, Lampe, and made a point of noting in his little book of wisdom that the name "Lampe" had to be forgotten, Goethe made no secret of his determination to stick with the name "Carl" right from the start.)

Providing hot chocolate was one of his servant's most exquisite tasks. Not only was Carl indispensable as a helper on trips when it came to keeping the luggage together; dealing with carriage drivers, innkeepers, and bedmaids; and caring for overcoats and suits, but he also had a vital role in collecting stones and other objects, taking dictation, copying paperwork, and keeping a diary and ledger—it was important to maintain an overview of the financial situation if His Excellency Goethe, the privy councilor and minister of state, should once again spend more money than budgeted. In short, Carl saw to all the errands that arose in the chaos of everyday life. Recorder, secretary, chocolatier . . . these activities merged seamlessly. Without his servant Carl, Goethe would have been in a bind, overburdened with the sheer universality of his universal duties.

Such matters were a breeze for Johann Jacob Ludwig Geist. In 1795, when he started working for Goethe, Geist already had a healthy dose of self-confidence, and in contrast to his predecessors, Paul Götze and Christoph Sutor—Götze had served the poet, minister of state, and natural scientist for a respectable seventeen years, and Sutor for nearly twenty—he had no need of meticulous training and instruction. Geist had worked in the field of education, was proficient in Latin, and had extensive knowledge of botany; he could even play the organ rather well. Schiller referred to him as "Goethe's valiant spirit," more like a Sancho Panza than a Wagner, Faust's scholarly assistant. Goethe had already promised him a civil service post in Weimar if he should ever wish to leave the job, as was the right and proper thing to do for a loyal squire.

All of them—Goethe, his servant, his coachman, and Schiller—were merry on this February day as they drew closer to Jena. Even the horses pulled the sleigh more quickly as they approached the mountains around the city, a crack of the whip filling the air.

She held her basket firmly clasped on her shoulder, the straps cutting into her flesh. Crisscrossed cords barely held together the goods and packages, which were on the verge of spilling out of the overflowing pannier. She wore a headscarf, a skirt, and an apron, and carried an additional woven willow basket in her hand for smaller items, such as fruits, herbs, and fresh vegetables. She was passing through the tiny village of Frankendorf, northwest of Jena, for the second time in a day. The surrounding villages were Umpferstedt, Kapellendorf, and Hammerstedt.

Spinster Wenzel (as she was known) took a break at the inn in Frankendorf before moving on in the early morning hours. She always stopped at the inn to set down her basket during her five-hour journey, especially at night, when it grew chilly.

Spinster Wenzel carried a heavy load; the basket could weigh a good fifty pounds. She transported private mail, medications, and everyday items twice a week. On Tuesdays and Fridays her path took her from Jena to Weimar, and she reversed course on Wednesdays and Saturdays. Even though mail transported on horseback could get through this route far more quickly, she held a clear advantage: she was able to deliver dispatches directly—people could receive replies to a letter they gave her as soon as the very next day. For the countrywomen who had no spare time during the harvest season, she bought household items and dishes at the market; she delivered medications for doctors and pharmacists, and goods to wealthy customers for businessmen. As payment, she generally received one-tenth of the value of the goods.

The ducal postal system would have liked to bar any competition, but the government was not receptive to such opposition. Weimar and Jena were virtually cut off from transregional communication, as they were not situated along the Via Regia, the central trade route of the Holy Roman Empire of the German Nation. Leipzig and Erfurt were key intersections. The nearest direct access was in Buttelstedt, north of Weimar, more than seven miles away. Women who served as couriers were an essential complement to stagecoaches, which traveled far too slowly anyway. Without them, large parts of the country would have been unable to receive postal deliveries.

On this day, Spinster Wenzel had especially important mail with her: letters from Herr Goethe to Herr Schiller. She had been ferrying their correspondence back and forth for quite some time, as well as the presents they exchanged. She was now coming from the house on Frauenplan, carrying a whole pike in her baggage. The stench of fish wafted behind her, and a good hundred yards ahead of her when the wind suddenly changed direction. She even had to transport stones from Goethe's collection to Jena, or pages from some journal packaged in an empty box she had previously used to carry Frau Schiller's homemade crackers to Weimar. Gifts, this way and that.

She often had to wait until the men had read a letter, formulated a reply, and found any materials they wished to add. But she was reliable. Particularly when time was of the essence, when final adjustments had to be made in advance of the premiere, the courier provided invaluable services. Ultimately, she was the one to determine the rhythm of the correspondence that maintained the exchange of ideas between Goethe and Schiller.

Spinster Wenzel took one last swallow from her jug. It was the break of day, and she had to make haste. Her path went by way of Hohlstedt and Isserstedt, down into the Mühltal, about one more mile, and then—Jena.

The time Goethe spent in Jena was beneficial not only to his literary work but also to his natural science studies. Plants, stones, clouds, bones—everything was in motion, everything was in perpetual transition, from the simple organisms up to the more complex forms, step by step, culminating in the most complex operation of all: inserting human beings into the whole of nature, the system of its individual members. Goethe attempted to furnish a new methodological basis for the separate areas of natural science. He called it morphology, "the study of the configuration, formation, and modification of organic forms."

Schiller played no small part in Goethe's ability to make such admirable progress in his studies of nature in Jena. Schiller functioned as a mirror, showing him things he would never have seen for himself.

The story of their friendship was the story of an enduring revolution. Their one basic conflict, over how experience and ideas were related, was debated over and over again. Like all beginnings, theirs was difficult. They had finally arrived at a resolution in 1794, in Jena, at a convention of the Society for Nature Research.

Goethe and Schiller, honorary members of the society, attended a lecture at the Bachstein House on Rathausgasse. Both were disappointed by the lecture; when Goethe wanted to leave the room early, Schiller stood up as well, and they met up at the exit as both squeezed through the narrow door. Then they unexpectedly launched into a conversation about how nature could be regarded in such a fragmented manner, and how it needed to be seen instead as an indivisible, organic whole—as life. And as they went outside, Goethe suddenly saw common ground between them: their interest in nature.

Schiller had opened wide the proverbial door, and Goethe stepped through, presenting his view of how nature needed to be construed as active and lively, expanding out of one whole into its component parts, and never as separate or isolated. They strolled down the street, passing the corner house across from the town hall where their mutual friend Wilhelm von Humboldt had just recently taken up residence, and walked the short distance across the market. This was nothing like their previous encounter.

Their first meeting, in September 1788 in Rudolstadt, had

been arranged by Charlotte von Lengefeld, Schiller's future wife. It did not go well. Goethe's expectations had been low as it was; he had despised Schiller's play *The Robbers*. At the time, Goethe, who had recently returned from a stay in Italy, was examining the metamorphosis of plants, the process by which seed developed into leaf, leaf into stem, stem into fruit, and, finally, fruit once again into seed and leaf. But just as he had failed to come across the archetype of all plants, which he was seeking while in Palermo's botanical garden, he also failed to secure any acknowledgment from natural scientists. Moreover, he felt that Schiller was not his ally either. His interest in getting to know him better had not grown in the interim.

By the time they arrived at Schiller's house, a fair amount of time had gone by—neither could say just how much—though Schiller lived close to Rathausgasse, a stone's throw from the lecture venue. Now they stood in front of it, still chatting away about nature and its relationship to science. Once again, Schiller opened the door, and once again Goethe stepped inside— literally, this time.

A quaint spiral staircase led up to the apartment. Just recently, Schiller had returned from his home in Swabia and moved out of the garden house on Zwätzengasse, where he had spent the past few months, and into the first and second floors of a grand three-floor faculty house. The gabled façade, which looked out onto the market square, had a simple design.

The apartment was spacious. The whitewashed walls were decorated with silhouettes, and the sofa and chairs were upholstered with striped fabric. There were still cups on the table; books and newspapers were scattered everywhere. And while Schiller settled down on the sofa with a sigh of relief about how their conversation had turned out, Goethe, with a sweeping motion of his arm, began to sketch his view of the metamorphosis of plants and trace the theory. Right then and there he created a symbolic plant in front of Schiller's eyes. Schiller, in turn, was filled with admiration and intense interest as he watched his fellow writer work his way into his speech. In the end, however, he came to the sober conclusion that it was not experience that Goethe had just sketched in the air: it was an idea. Goethe stopped short. The point on which they were divided had been identified. They would need to map it out. Goethe retorted that he was quite pleased to have ideas without even knowing it; his ideas could even be visualized! Schiller realized that he had to agree. Neither emerged as the victor. In other situations, the two of them liked to present themselves as insuperable authorities, but not now, not with the sort of counterpart each presented to the other. The difference between them had been set in stone. Each of them now saw his own position far more clearly from the standpoint of the other.

They had taken a crucial step forward. Having hit it off extraordinarily well, they each expressed the hope that they would see the other more often in the future and continue to exchange experiences and ideas. After that unexpected encounter, it appeared that neither could imagine going on without the other; working in tandem created a productive tension and focused their energy. Since that day, the conversation had continued nonstop, and they came together as Goethe *and* Schiller, acting on equal footing. From that time on, Jena was right around the corner from Weimar.

To Schlegel or
to Be Schlegeled

LITERARY DEVILRIES

After an extended period of not knowing what to do with him-
self or having an idea of his place in the world, Clemens Brentano developed distinct views about life. Even though he was
only twenty years old, he had made up his mind: He had no
intention of becoming a merchant or an attorney or a physician.
He had higher goals. He intended to write a novel and bring out
the genius that he felt was slumbering within him.

Since opting against a conventional career, he'd spent more
and more time at Caroline Schlegel's lunch gatherings, and broke
off contact with his fellow students. He now associated with different people, which felt like compensation for the unreasonable
daily demands he had to put up with in the sleepy school setting.
At the Schlegels', Brentano—who was officially matriculated as
a student of medicine—met Schelling, the renowned philosopher; Paulus, the theologian; the translator Gries, who had come
from Göttingen for a visit; Tieck, who was spending the winter
in Jena with his wife; Johann Wilhelm Ritter, the well-known

natural scientist; and the Schelling apologist Henrik Steffens. At times there were some fifteen to eighteen people at the table.

Caroline had her hands full tending to her guests. Sometimes she had no idea what she could put on the table even as the clock struck twelve, and she would make do with boiled potatoes and sour herring, or a thin stew if there was nothing else on hand. She improvised as well as she could. But Brentano and the others were not coming for the food; they came for the conversation, which focused on literature or the latest developments in natural science or philosophy, and on Kant, again and again. Caroline always knew how to get the conversation moving again when it faltered.

The level of creativity ran high. Ideas sprang to mind and faded away. Time melted like a pat of butter in a pan. Only Gries—or "Griesette," the nickname Caroline used to call him to attention at the lunch table when he was daydreaming as usual—remained strikingly silent. More went into his mouth than came out, even though he was quite a gregarious fellow, a writer and translator who was actually more the latter, especially from the Romance languages; to date, he had translated Dante, Ariosto, Tasso, and Calderón into German. No one—with the possible exception of Wilhelm—could measure up to him in this arena.

Today the group was taking aim at one of its favorite targets. In his new play, August von Kotzebue had mounted a frontal attack on the Schlegels. Kotzebue, a decidedly mediocre dramatist whose vanity led him to conclude that he was on a par with Goethe and Schiller just because his plays were more successful in Germany, had decided to tackle the Schlegels head on. The play, called *The Hyperborean Donkey, or Today's Education*, was greeted in Jena with derisive laughter: "To be or not to be—*I* or *not-I*—to Schlegel or to be Schlegeled: that is the question."

One scene, devoted to the *Athenaeum*, had Fritz end up in a madhouse.

The texts in the *Athenaeum*, shot through with ingenuity, carried a tinge of pretentiousness and crudeness in Kotzebue's rendering. Kotzebue's hatred for the Schlegel circle ran deep. He accused its members of being incomprehensible, pretentious, and inspired by a revolutionary spirit, and he invoked all the various reproaches that typified the feelings of Berlin Enlightenment circles. The Merkels and the Nicolais got in on the mudslinging act. Garlieb Merkel was said to have gone around Berlin claiming that the duke had reprimanded the Schlegels for their work in the *Athenaeum*. That very evening, Wilhelm and Tieck cobbled together a polemical sonnet to Merkel, which included these lines:

> *Did you come from faraway Latvia in a frame of mind*
> *To splash about in the filth of mankind?*
> *Go back to your fatherland to make your mess.*
> *Journals, with Garlieb Merkel, don't acquiesce!*

The *Allgemeine Literatur-Zeitung* also plotted and schemed against the Schlegels and published scathing reviews. Once a leading voice on the subject of Kantianism and a weapon in the fight against dogmatism, the journal turned into a stronghold of resentment as the years went by. At any rate, the hostility was mutual, and Wilhelm, who had already written close to three hundred reviews for the *Allgemeine Literatur-Zeitung*, planned to part ways with the publication.

They could hardly contain their laughter about Kotzebue's "donkey play." Even Fritz, the intended target of Kotzebue's ridicule, found it enormously entertaining: "And what is a donkey? the wise man asks. A finite thing with infinite ears." At some point liqueur was served. Who cared what the world thought, if all you wanted was to choose your own individual path in life? Brentano happily offered a toast. *Santé!* The world at large did nothing but clog up the streets anyway.

One man in Jena was roundly disliked by the attendees of the lunch gatherings. Whenever the name Friedrich Schiller came up in conversation, people rolled their eyes. This was a bit unpleasant for Wilhelm, for Schiller had been the one to invite him and Caroline to come to Jena in 1795. Chatting in person would be far more pleasant than writing letters, Schiller had told him.

The letter had reached him by way of Friedrich Körner, Schiller's friend and benefactor, in Amsterdam, where he had been working as a tutor since 1791 in what was intended as a six-year arrangement—a largely unedifying period in his studies.

There were no public libraries in Amsterdam, at least none worthy of the name, and he had no access to private ones. Fritz sent him new releases and excerpts on occasion. But libraries were a necessity; he would not be able to get his writing done without them. Wilhelm had the easiest access to the works of the ancient Greeks and Romans, because the pupil he was instructing, Willem Ferdinand Mogge Muilman, was the only son of the wealthy merchant and financier Henric Muilman, who had also made a name for himself as an art collector. Henric owned close to two hundred paintings. The walls of his residence on Herengracht, where Wilhelm also lived, displayed many of them, including Vermeer's *The Milkmaid* and *The Lacemaker*, and a portrait of Elisabeth Bas that was attributed to Rembrandt.

Wilhelm led a comfortable life in Amsterdam. Muilman's

business connections extended to India and South America. Unloaded daily at the harbor were goods from faraway, exotic-sounding countries, quite a few of which were delivered to the Muilman residence. Wilhelm lacked for nothing, at least in the material sense, although the tortoise pâté was a disappointment—neither fish nor fowl.

In order to advance in the scholarly world, he began to translate from Dutch, a language he considered utterly graceless and devoid of poetry, somewhat like Low German, a provincial dialect that was almost an affront to the ear of a philologist trained at the esteemed University of Göttingen. He worked on a book about the Anglo-Dutch Naval Wars, a thankless task devoid of interest to anyone outside the academic world. In the end, the book, *Communications to Clarify the Events During the Last War Between England and Holland*, was published under a pseudonym. It was nothing to brag about.

And so Wilhelm was greatly delighted to receive Schiller's invitation to Jena. Samples of his Dante translation were already slated for publication in *Die Horen*, in the absence of any direct contact with Schiller; the arrangements were made by his brother, Fritz. The unembellished opening lines of the first canto of Dante's *Inferno* were felicitous:

> *Als ich die Bahn des Lebens halb vollendet*
> *Fand ich in einem dunklen Walde mich*
> *Weil ich vom graden Weg mich abgewendet.* *

---

* When I had journeyed half of our life's way,
   I found myself within a shadowed forest,
   for I had lost the path that does not stray.
The Divine Comedy of Dante Alighieri: The Inferno: A Verse Translation, trans. and ed. Allen Mandelbaum (New York: Bantam, 1982), 3.

Dante spoke to all the eras, all the events that had occurred since his day, even though they had yet to take place.

Jena seemed a promising place to stir up the world of literature. Goethe, Schiller, Fichte—Wilhelm had heard a great deal about their world, and now he had established contact with it.

Schiller thought highly of the Schlegel brothers in their capacity as distinguished experts in German and European literature, as equally brilliant translators, particularly of the Shakespeare dramas, and as profound philologists. Since 1789, when Wilhelm had come out with his earliest attempts at translating Shakespeare, the project of a German Shakespeare translation had taken on an increasingly distinct shape. It started with *A Midsummer Night's Dream*, then moved on to *Romeo and Juliet*— and there was a great deal still to be done even after *Hamlet*. One of Schiller's major reasons for wishing to establish a relationship with the two brothers was his work for many journal projects, including *Thalia, Die Horen, Musen-Almanach*, and his contributions to the *Allgemeine Literatur-Zeitung*; these journals were read throughout Germany, and the work enabled Schiller to make ends meet.

By 1799, there was not a trace left of their initial affinity and common ground. Wilhelm was annoyed by Schiller's repeated invitations to contribute poems to the *Musen-Almanach*, and told Goethe to feel free to submit to Schiller some of the "little poems" Wilhelm had sent him; considering their strained relationship, Wilhelm wrote, he could hardly believe that Schiller had meant his invitation seriously. The matter was buried.

People eagerly conversed with Goethe, and just as eagerly made fun of Schiller. His poem "The Song of the Bell" had become a source of great amusement shortly after its publication in the *Musen-Almanach* for the year 1800, and the text was picked to pieces. People almost fell off their chairs laughing at the dreadfulness of the words Schiller had put down on paper. The poem was grandiloquent, outmoded, and passé, nineteen rickety stanzas riddled with all kinds of drivel crammed into cockeyed images:

> *Women, to hyenas turning,*
> *Carry on their shocking jests*
> *And quivering still, panthers' teeth burning,*
> *Rip apart their enemies' breasts.*

That was Schiller's vision of revolution. The opening lines wormed their way into people's heads, and there was simply no forgetting that first stanza: "Walled up fast within the earth / Stands the mold burned out of clay . . ." It could drive people mad.

In comparison with Goethe, Schiller was just too staid, too somber. No sooner had Schiller written the poem "The Dignity of Women"—also an object of ridicule—than Wilhelm hastened to pen a parody, "Schiller's Praise of Women," as the only coping mechanism he could come up with:

> *Honor to women! They knit the socks,*
> *Woolly and warm, for wading through swamps,*
> *Patch up ragged pantaloons.*

Given years, Schiller would not be able to create a text on the level of something Goethe could produce in a single afternoon.

Still, they had to make sure that these lampoons were not seen by the wrong eyes over in Weimar. Nothing would be worse than that: Mocking Schiller openly would imperil their personal bond with Goethe, and the Schlegel circle placed a higher value on a friendly relationship with Goethe than on any literary devilries.

The meal was over, and the guests got up and went back to their desks. Brentano headed off to see Sophie Mereau, a poet who was eight years his senior and married to a professor who lived on Jenergasse, just a stone's throw from Leutragasse. This, too, was a new habit of his. He spent several hours a day in her company.

The group spread out among the various floors of the house: Dorothea downstairs, Caroline one flight up, then Wilhelm, and Fritz on the top floor, under the roof. They agreed to meet up for an afternoon stroll. Only Wilhelm stayed at home. He would be taking a walk again the following day with Goethe, who had arranged with the duke to extend his leave. The particularly knotty passages of the following year's new edition of the *Roman Elegies* still needed to be worked out. The greatest living poet was in need of an extra dose of classicism, and of all the places he could have chosen to go, he headed straight to this group, the "wasps' nest."

These walks, which took place every morning from ten o'clock to one, were excessively long. Each time Wilhelm returned from a morning stroll with Goethe at Paradise, a large park adjacent to the Saale River, back and forth along the two avenues of linden trees, he felt as though his legs were falling off. Sprawled out on the sofa afterward, he listened to Fritz going up and down the stairs.

The Old Man
from the Mountain

IN PARADISE WITH GOETHE

Tieck wished to be read not by just anyone, but by the master from Weimar himself. In early December, when Goethe traveled to Jena for another visit, the time had come for Tieck to introduce him to his newly completed *Genoveva*. In this work, Tieck cast the medieval legend of the same name—a celebration of religion, chivalry, and courtly love—as a drama. Someone whose own era has turned its back on him can also turn his back on the era, and look instead to the past, not necessarily with an eye toward reverting to it, but more as a means of regaining stability by engaging in inward reflection. The story of Countess Genoveva, who is sentenced to death for alleged infidelity yet doesn't lose confidence and belief in a higher destiny, surely brought solace to readers in Tieck's fraught era.

Fritz, Novalis, and the others already knew about *Genoveva*. A month earlier Tieck had recited it to them at a gathering, and his friends were buzzing with excitement. It was a sensation in the close-knit circle. Wilhelm Heinrich Wackenroder's religious sensibility, Friedrich Schleiermacher's intuition and feeling,

Jakob Böhme's wondrous mysticism: The work brimmed with literary references and philosophical allusions, and the audience easily grasped what he was after. Tieck was relieved.

Up to this point he had focused on folktales, novels, and essays on art theory, nothing that would ordinarily be characterized as drama. He was known for *Bluebeard, Franz Sternbald's Journeying Years,* and the *Outpourings of an Art-Loving Friar.* He had written and then anonymously published his essays with his friend Wackenroder. But Wackenroder had succumbed a year earlier to typhus, a hellish illness, and since then Tieck had been seeking connections to the literary world. He felt that in the house on Leutragasse he had found what he was looking for.

He had been in the city since the summer. In mid-October, his wife, Amalie, and their little daughter, Dorothea, who was less than half a year old, had followed him there. If he had the choice, they would all stay until at least the spring.

Tieck was now a regular at Caroline's lunch group, "sympoeticizing" with his new friends, and in the evenings he read aloud from his own dramas and poems. He was welcome in the little cosmos of this house, where, at times, as though by sheer coincidence, the whole world seemed to be flourishing.

Tieck appreciated these friendships, but he could not bear to hear the feuds; the constant railing about Kotzebue, the *Allgemeine Literatur-Zeitung,* and Merkel; the endless back-and-forth between Caroline and Schelling. He would sit there in silence and wait for it to be over. If he were not such close friends with the group's members, he might well have written a comedy about them by now: he had enough material to draw on. The very idea that Dorothea Veit had now begun to write a novel on top of everything—how very tasteless!

Still, Novalis and Wilhelm contacted Weimar on Tieck's behalf, giving him the opening he needed to visit Goethe. Tieck saw that Goethe took to him immediately. Now the master would finally get to know him from a literary point of view, in detail, with a text of a very different caliber—not a fairy tale or a novel, but a tragedy in five acts.

Tieck had longed for this moment since his youth. His entire life had seemed to be aimed at meeting and impressing Goethe, and now he could picture putting on a play in Weimar under Goethe's direction.

They arranged to meet in the evening, on the top floor of the Stadtschloss in Jena. The servant, Carl, had left for the night, and they were alone. Goethe sat in his easy chair, a cup of hot chocolate in front of him, his legs tucked into a blanket. They chatted about this and that, mostly about Shakespeare. Tieck asked Goethe how he had liked Ben Jonson, whom Tieck had recommended to him a few months earlier in Weimar. Next to Shakespeare, Jonson was arguably the most important drama-tist of his time, that great century of the Renaissance. *What a rascal, a real devil of a fellow with all kinds of tricks up his sleeve, yes, indeed, quite the ladykiller.* And while Goethe tried to dodge the question—he had only skimmed Jonson's work—it suddenly struck Tieck that he was seeing Götz, Faust, Tasso, and all the other characters in Goethe's dramas reflected in the writer's facial features. He was having the same reaction as Dorothea, who had recently told him about her own vivid encounter with Goethe in the park.

Then Tieck was given the signal to begin, and as he read, slowly finding his way into the text, Goethe listened attentively and immersed himself in every sentence. It seemed as though the play needed to be read aloud to highlight its dramatic quality, and to be complete. The room filled with the voice of Tieck, who proved once again how gifted a reciter he was, a true "reading machine," as Caroline, Wilhelm, Fritz, and Dorothea already knew full well. The acoustical component enhanced and fleshed out the text:

> *How he gives shape to his creations, I can't say*
> *No tongue can tell the things I've felt*
> *The earthly breath dare not express today*
> *What angels sang to make the hard heart melt*
> *And as the spring begins to hold the gloom at bay*
> *Of tough, bleak winter with which we've dealt*
> *The spring springs forth, to our delight*
> *And one more blossom wends its way out, fresh and bright.*

Dorothea feared that she would not be seeing Goethe again. Everyone else knew him, and some had known him for quite a long time. Caroline had first met Goethe twenty years earlier in Göttingen, and Wilhelm took walks with him almost every day through Paradise Park. But Dorothea? Not seeing Goethe would be disgraceful; it would be like going to Rome and not kissing the Pope's slippers. Tieck had just recently told her that it would be better to get together with Goethe in Jena, where he behaved quite differently from the way he acted back at home in Weimar. But whenever Goethe came to Jena, he was always with Schiller, and people were saying that Schiller had decided to leave Jena. Dorothea was not at all pleased. Although she could not stand Schiller any better than the others could, Goethe might never show up again if Schiller were to move to Weimar.

But now, as she walked along the river with her friends to recover from a speech that Novalis had just inflicted on them— posing the idea of a new Christianity, the vision of a reborn community of Catholics and Protestants from the spirit of the

Middle Ages—Dorothea thought she could make out somebody under the bright afternoon sky dotted with puffy clouds. She was taken aback. Hadn't Novalis just stated that nothing was more indispensable to true piety than an intermediary that connects us with God, his manifestation in the flesh?

As Dorothea dashed along, Fritz was barely able to keep up with her. She had left the rest of the group a good distance behind, given the slip to Tieck and Wilhelm, and Novalis and his brother Karl plodded behind the others in a daze. Goethe attempted to evade the big crowd heading toward him, but it was too late. He gave a quick glance to the group, and compliments were exchanged. How nice it would be for Dorothea to be alone with him now.

At first she could not bring herself to say anything to him. But, figuring it was better to speak than to have no conversation at all, she came up with a steady stream of chatter, settling on the topic of the torrents of the Saale and the river rafts.

Goethe proved more affable than she had been led to believe from the others' stories. He even accompanied her back up the mountain from which he had just come down. He walked beside her with an even, rather heavy stride, his hands clasped behind his back. And while he launched into a lecture about the particulars of the region, the course of the Saale River, and the work of raftsmen, Dorothea, who had grown up in the Goethe cult of the Berlin salons—Friedrich Nicolai had called her and the other female salongoers "Goethe slaves"—had trouble keeping her mind on what he was telling her. All of the poems of his that she knew by heart sprang to mind, as did the title character in his novel *Wilhelm Meister*, whom, as she now thought, Goethe even resembled somewhat. She now began to imagine that *all* the characters in his writings were reflected in his eyes: Götz von Berlichingen, Faust, Tasso. If only he were not so corpulent.

Giulio Romano, *Olympus*, ceiling fresco in the Palazzo del Te, Mantua,
1526–1535 (detail)

Goethe had grown so fat—bloated, actually—that he looked like a Frankfurt wine merchant.

After half an hour, which seemed like an eternity to Dorothea, their chat came to an end. When she took his hand to say good-bye, sweat was dripping down his chin like watery soup.

The silence in the room was finally broken by the midnight chimes, resounding like a distant roll of thunder. It was already late at night when Tieck laid the manuscript aside. Both of them had lost track of the time.

The hot chocolate on the table in front of Goethe had grown cold, and a skin had formed over the milk. Through the window, which was open just a crack, he could hear the clock tower chiming. Not just ten or eleven, but midnight. The only truth to be had was that which resisted, unchanging, the tyranny of current trends and their way of revolving around themselves.

They had sat together for four hours, with nothing between them but Tieck's voice and the text of *Genoveva*. They had no choice but to postpone the second part for the following evening, even though Goethe had already said that they would not be alone the next day, as August, his nine-year-old son, would be joining them. Goethe suggested a few revisions, though not many; he liked the play. The young author would take them to heart.

Tieck said good night; he, too, seemed exhausted. He went out into the cold night air and heard the students singing as they made their way home from the taverns.

Intermezzo

What an exhilarating thought: a change of century was immi-
nent, the beginning of a new era. From the impact of the gun-
shots, to the words engraved on invitations, to the sermons
delivered at church—great attention was paid to every detail in
those days. It was startling to contemplate that the seven was
passing into the eight.

In scholarly circles, a dispute erupted over the question of
when the new era, the new century, would actually begin: On
January 1, 1800? Or was the year 1800 still part of the old era?
This controversy was debated in the royal courts and all around
town. The one side believed that the watershed moment occurred as soon as the year 1800 could be written on stationery
letterhead, while the other insisted that people needed to bide
their time until 1801, that the turn of the century was more
than a calligraphic event.

The "nullists" couldn't believe what they were hearing: What,
"1"? The 8 was the crux! Eighteen hundred clearly started with
an 8, and by one year later, one's fingers would be well accus-
tomed to writing it, one's mouth to saying "eighteen hundred."
Couldn't anyone with half a brain and an appreciation of the

fundamental crossroads in life see that with the twelve chimes on December 31, 1799, a once-in-a-lifetime turning point would be reached?

Arguments of this kind did not sway those on the other side, who countered with an entirely different sort of nitpicking. If the nullists' point of view and logic were correct, a person with a debt of 300 thalers would need to pay back only 299. Anyone who regarded the year 1800 itself as part of the new century would also have to count the 300th thaler as part of the following set of hundred years, and hence the amount owed would have to be reduced accordingly. The nineteenth century would plainly be cheating the eighteenth out of a thaler. Could that really be regarded as historical justice?

The debate went back and forth in this manner. One year earlier, in the *Göttinger Taschenkalender*, Georg Christoph Lichtenberg had published his "Speech by the Numeral 8," held in the (fictitious) plenary council of numerals. The council, district, and committee "president" is the zero, the placeholder of eternity.

The aim is to resolve the issue of when the birthday for the nineteenth century can be celebrated: on the day the numeral 8 steps into the hundreds column (that is, on the first day of the year 1800) or—a full year later—when the numeral 1 takes its place in the ones column, marking the beginning of the year 1801? The question is of great interest to the numeral 8; after all, the question of the first year of its reign in the hundreds column, an honor not often bestowed, is at stake. The 8 had last occupied that spot nine hundred years earlier, just as much time as had passed between the beginning of recorded time and the end of its first time in office. Its heart bleeds at the thought of assuming office during the old century, rather than at the commencement of the new century, in which the number of planets will double, and the number of satellites and metals quadruple, in which the ratio of the battles between nations waged in the air to the older battles fought on land and at sea will be 580 to 1, in which newspaper correspondents from Paris and Hamburg will point their multifooted telescopes heavenward and watch the heroes and their rhapsodists—zooming high above like birds of prey and skylarks—fall from the sky.

The question of a century's beginning date was older than the dispute being carried on at the time. A hundred years earlier, in the large neighboring state of Prussia, when stances on this issue were similarly entrenched, the decision was made to have the eighteenth century begin on January 1, 1701, if for no other reason than that the court in Berlin wanted to have the coronation of the king and ascent of Brandenburg be regarded as a signal of a new era, a new century. The first heroic deed of the eighteenth century: the establishment of an entire kingdom, with Friedrich I at its head. On January 1, 1801, the hundredth anniversary of the Prussian coronation would be commemorated, with King Friedrich Wilhelm III and Queen Luise at its head. The Roman Curia had voted for 1701 as well. In France, on the other hand, where the French revolutionary calendar had been used for the past eight years, virtually nobody cared about this issue. France was in the middle of Nivôse, the "snow month," Year VIII of the Republic, the eighth year in which liberty, equality, and fraternity had become the bywords on French soil.

The nullists were overpowered this time as well, and had to defer to the arguments of the opposing side. To complete the hundred, the hundred itself had to be there already. The twelve measured chimes at midnight had yet to proclaim the start of a new century; the century was deferred.

History Is Made

The boxes were packed and the crates loaded, but the upcoming move was only one reason the past few weeks had been grueling for the Schillers. Lolo had given birth in October. The child— named Caroline—was healthy, but her mother had lost quite a bit of blood. Bedridden and racked by fever, she had been in such critical condition that the doctor nearly gave up on her. But now she was on the mend. It had been unfathomable to contemplate her not surviving the birth of her baby.

When Schiller moved from his urban apartment on Löbder-graben to his garden house at the Leutra River, he was already weighing another move—to Weimar, in hopes of enjoying better air quality and more exercise, and, in large part, in order to be closer to Goethe and the theater. In the spring, *Wallenstein's Death*, the third and final part of the Wallenstein drama, had been performed to great acclaim, and in July it was even lauded by the Prussian royal couple, who had flatly refused to attend the production in Berlin—only Weimar was worth consider-ing. The duke expressed a wish for Schiller to settle down per-manently in Weimar, ideally before the end of the year, before the winter. And now his third child had arrived. Charlotte von

Kalb, who had known Schiller when he was still a penniless playwright in Mannheim, offered the family her fully furnished apartment on Windischengasse.

So it was back to the court, the very milieu he had fled so many years earlier in Württemberg. He could still vividly recall that night in 1782, when he suddenly saw a way to break free of Duke Karl Eugen. While the duke was holding a celebration to honor the Russian Grand Duke Paul and his wife, a niece of the duke, the entire city was in an uproar, with distinguished people as far as the eye could see, fireworks in the night sky over Stuttgart, at Solitude Palace. Schiller was a military physician, but he was determined to become a writer at long last, a *full-time* writer, no matter what it took to achieve that goal. How could people write literature in a land where they were perpetually denied freedom of thought? Amid all the excitement surrounding the celebration he could—and did—slip away unnoticed. He had a friend, Andreas Streicher, who was heading to Hamburg to study the piano with the renowned Carl Philipp Emanuel Bach. Schiller himself wanted to go to Mannheim. He had once made his way there in the past, for the premiere of his play *The Robbers*. Next, he intended to present his latest play, *Fiesco's Conspiracy at Genoa*, to Wolfgang Heribert von Dalberg, the artistic director of the Mannheim National Theater.

Adieu, farewell. And now it was time for him to leave again. Off he went to Weimar, to Goethe, back into the arms of the duke.

Nothing was left to chance, absolutely nothing. Schelling won the first trick during his regular Saturday get-together with Schiller and Niethammer, where they played a card game called ombre, said to have been invented in fourteenth-century Spain. The game had such an array of variants that it was hard for them to agree on the rules at first.

Schelling did not say much while he played; he constantly fiddled with his handkerchief, then coolly plunked his cards down on the table. He and Schiller barely had anything to say to each other anymore. The enthusiasm with which Schelling had rushed to see him the very day of his arrival had ebbed. By now they were seeing each other only to play cards or when they were both meeting with Goethe, even though, as Schiller himself once had to concede, this limited contact was a "shame for philosophy."

Apart from card games, Goethe was the sole interest they still had in common. When the three got together, they generally spoke about natural science in general and magnetism in particular. They had also recently discussed Schleiermacher's speeches, collected in the volume *On Religion*. At first, Goethe praised these speeches to the skies, but once he realized that the emphasis was increasingly Christian toward the end of the volume, he firmly dismissed them.

At their previous gathering they had gone page by page through Schelling's introduction to the *First Outline of a System of the Philosophy of Nature*. The text demanded Goethe's full attention. There was a tremendous amount of new material on every page. At any rate, while Schiller remained oddly silent, Goethe was able to win over Schelling to his own approach. The world soul and the concept of metamorphosis were gradually converging. This was a minor triumph, even though Schelling knew that Goethe distrusted philosophy, particularly the idealism that predominated in Jena.

For his part, Schiller was staging a play every now and then. His new drama, *Mary Stuart*, was a tragedy in five acts. Like his

Wallenstein trilogy, this drama drew on rich historical material. He had already completed the first act, and the second would soon follow. But work on the *Musen-Almanach* was now taking up all of Schiller's time. A little card-playing diversion might be just the thing.

When Schiller and Niethammer got up from the card table, Schelling was jovial for a change. He had won again and again, even the final round. Nothing was left to chance for someone with enough imagination to anticipate the various courses the game could take, and to play his trump card at just the right moment.

Schiller and his family left Jena on December 3, 1799. They were departing for good. He could no longer picture himself returning for anything more than a quick visit. His bonds with Goethe, with Weimar, and with the duke would be long-lasting.

No other place would ever be as meaningful to him as Jena and its environs. He had formed very strong ties since he first stepped foot in the college town more than twelve years earlier. The inaugural lecture at the Griesbach Auditorium, which took place in 1789, one year after his arrival, had been met with such great fanfare. The title of the lecture was itself poetic: "What Is Universal History, and for What Purpose Is It Studied?" He clearly recalled the moment of entering the lecture hall, in the immediate vicinity of the Stadtschloss, to which they had moved the event once his predecessor Reinhold's auditorium proved to be too small.

Looking out the window, he had watched group after group coming up the street, with no end in sight. Fortunately, a brother-in-law of Griesbach was in the audience. The suggestion was

Albrecht Dürer, *Nemesis (The Great Fortune)*, 1501–1502

made to change the venue to a different auditorium, and the spectacle began: Everyone raced down Johannisgasse, one of Jena's longest streets, now crammed full of students. People ran as fast as their legs would carry them to get a good seat. The whole city was in a state of pandemonium.

After a short while, Schiller, accompanied by Reinhold, had followed the stream of students and entered the courtyard of the building. Crowding, jostling, pushing, and shoving ensued. Windowsills, vestibule, and hallway filled up all the way to the front door. It was the storming of the Salana.

Schiller spoke about the problem of history, about his own place in that history. The present, woven from the threads of the past, pointed toward an open future that had yet to be crafted. The pointless game of *Fatum, Nemesis, Fortuna* was over. History was produced, wittingly or unwittingly. There was no providence determining whether the human race was moving forward or backward. Giambattista Vico had expressed this idea in his *New Science* in the early part of the eighteenth century: Nothing lasts forever; the truth is created, and history along with it.

Schiller's words, like the storming of the Bastille, left indelible traces on those present, who found they were witnessing the dawn of a new era. Old-school metaphysics was being turned on its head, and ultimately had no choice but to capitulate. With Schiller, the new era gained, for the first time, a consciousness of itself as a present day emanating from the totality of the past, but with a wide-open horizon facing an unresolved future.

Back in his attic study in 1799, he stood gazing at the landscape one last time. He had spent so many evenings at the garden parapet of late, often retreating there to work without interruption. Schiller had the ceiling decorated with a view of the sky, complete with branches and birds. This was his summer palace.

He held his snuffbox, which was adorned with a mother-of-pearl disc and a gold-plated ring in the center of the lid. It had been a gift from his father. The rotten apples he sniffed whenever he was upset—a unique habit he had developed—would be staying behind in the drawer of his standing desk.

Vexing the Evangelists

NOVALIS AND THE RELIGION OF THE FUTURE

There is one kind of sociability for the summer, and another for the winter. Fritz, Wilhelm, Dorothea, and Caroline spent their evenings gathered in the parlor. The second, smaller sofa, which had been a gift from Carl Friedrich Ernst Frommann, the publisher, was positioned right in front of the fireplace.

Tieck moved up close to the tiles. Repeated flare-ups of rheumatism had made his life quite difficult, and the warmth did him good. Fritz, whose chair was farthest from the fire, kept blowing into his hands, then rubbing them together quickly.

The winter had been extraordinarily harsh. Their lack of money for wood and other supplies was compounded by a lack of trust. In the rift between Caroline and her husband over Caroline's dalliance with Schelling, Fritz took Wilhelm's side. His disappointment ran deep. He had remained discreet for quite a long time, but at some point he could no longer hold back; this was, after all, his brother's life. Dorothea, too, felt deceived by Caroline; it irked her that she had been taken in by this consummate hostess, in the evenings and at the lunch table, that she had put up with everything without saying a word. She had been overly grateful for the warm welcome she had received.

Wilhelm tried to mediate to keep the fronts from hardening; whatever had occurred between Caroline and himself had done nothing to change his love for her. He knew that she didn't love him, and never really had, not even when he had helped her in her hour of need, after the business in Mainz; he had even arranged for her to get poison in prison so she could put an end to her daughter's life and her own if she saw no other solution. He also knew that he was making himself look ridiculous in front of the others, that force of habit and weakness were keeping him tied to her, yet he still welcomed any caresses, kind words, or orders she directed his way. But neither of them made an attempt to clear the air or let off steam.

Perhaps Fritz took greater umbrage at the liaison than Wilhelm, who was directly affected by it, because Schelling had always been a thorn in his side. Or was it because Fritz would have liked to marry Caroline if his brother hadn't done so? Would everything have turned out differently in that case? He didn't know the answer himself.

The parlor would not warm up this evening, because the wood had been rationed. When the last log was thrown into the stove, the fire blazed up.

Since the previous year in Dresden, when the group had made its way through the antiquities collection by torchlight, they had not taken the time for a gathering that would run this long. Now Fritz and Dorothea, Wilhelm and Caroline, Novalis and his brother Karl, Schelling, Tieck, and the physicist Ritter had signed on for a multiday meeting. New texts would be read and discussed: religion and Holberg, Galvanism and poetry. This would be a colorful mix.

To make the guests feel at home, Caroline and Dorothea prepared for the event by turning the house upside down. They didn't even make it to the performance of Wilhelm's *Hamlet* translation in Berlin. Everything was laundered, twenty curtains mounted, the sofa reupholstered—they worked until they were ready to drop.

Caroline was missing her dear child, Gustel. Was she still a child? She had become more like a sister. Auguste was precocious: At the age of twelve, she had studied Greek and was reading Cervantes and Shakespeare. She was an indispensable confidante; without her, Caroline would have lost her mind back in Mainz. Gustel had traveled to Dessau, about eighty-five miles from Jena, to spend several weeks with the Tischbeins: Sophie, who had stayed with them earlier in Jena; her two daughters, Caroline and Betty; and her son, Carl. The girls' time together was raucous but magical; the rooms were messy, but their faces were radiant. They made music together—Caroline and Betty performed arias, and there were duets and trios with Auguste. Those had been carefree days. Now Auguste would be away until Christmas, but as always she left her heart with her mother. Caroline pulled herself together as well as she could.

The house was almost unrecognizable—the parlor swept clean, the rooms tidied up and spick-and-span, white curtains on the windows—when Novalis and his brother Karl arrived on November 11. They had just come from their sister Caroline's wedding to Friedrich von Rechenberg in Schlöben, a few miles outside Jena. The estate belonged to the family and was passed down to the firstborn from one generation to the next. Novalis, the eldest brother, had proposed the wedding toast, as a matter of honor.

Schlöben was an unnerving place for Novalis. Everything there reminded him of Sophie von Kühn, his late fiancée. Shortly after meeting her at Schloss Grüning, near Tennstedt, where he held his first appointment after studying the law in Leipzig, Novalis—head over heels in love—had posted a fictitious notice announcing that he would be wed to the then twelve-year-old Sophie in Schlöben on March 25, 1798, one week after her sixteenth birthday. By that day, she was no longer alive. A malignant liver disease had brought her life to an end a year earlier. What remained, however, was the infinite idea of love, and this pained him still. All the to-do surrounding his sister's nuptials was a constant reminder of his own wedding that might have been.

In this frame of mind, Novalis arrived at Leutragasse, where he had stopped off for a few days back in July and again in September. Now he did not have a wedding toast in his luggage; he would be speaking about Christianity, about a new religion for the future.

When his stifling speech ended, anxious whispering filled the room. The audience had expected something different, something more. Novalis's presentation sounded like a return to a bygone era. After all the years of revolutionary wars, there was finally a stable peace once again; only religion, Novalis contended, could awaken Europe, and not just any religion, but a Christianity that had moved beyond the disastrous discord between Protestantism and Catholicism. History, which now lay in tatters, would culminate in a "true Catholic" age.

Novalis was a visionary, a prophet who attempted to render possible the impossible, to depict the absolute, to bring harmony to an era torn apart by conflict, all through the power of his speech. And for him, speaking meant preaching, intoning his message near and far. All of history was a single gospel, and he its herald.

Schleiermacher's much-discussed *On Religion* speeches had inspired Novalis. Fritz had raved to him about the book, and in mid-September Novalis began to read it, finishing the text on the same day that Napoleon overthrew the Directory in a coup and made himself consul for life, the absolute ruler of the First Republic of France. A historical milestone: In Jena, the spirit of a new Christianity was being presented to the world, while over there, the legacy of the French Revolution was dissolving in the hands of a usurper. Freedom or despotism. For Novalis, there was no doubt that a new religion would arise, and with it a new era.

Schelling regarded the speech as a massive step backward. It brought to mind everything he had left behind in Tübingen years earlier: the old superstitions, traditional notions of immediacy, along with all manner of dogmas, which invariably had God appearing as a discrete individual being, sitting on his throne in heaven. Schelling grew more and more dismayed as he listened to Novalis's speech. Hadn't Kant made it plain, once and for all, that the existence of God could be neither proved nor refuted, and hence could be only an ideal, a limiting concept for the faculty of reason? Novalis had not presented a diagnosis of the current era as it stood on the threshold to a new age, but had instead opted for a cowardly escape route into the past.

Tieck, who otherwise saw eye to eye with Novalis, also found the speech half-baked and its conclusions arbitrary. Novalis had dived deep into the world of the Middle Ages in order to look beyond the present into a future no longer marked by the rifts produced by the Reformation and the fragmentation ensuing from the political revolution in France. In this future there would be only *one* Christianity, *one* overarching common interest, *one* sovereign. His historical overview showed the times gone by and their demons, the Church's suppression of the sciences, reintegrated into the larger course of history. Novalis had inserted himself directly into the Golden Age, yet how could he simply skate over the upheavals in these revolutionary times and herald the arrival of a new Messiah who would drive mankind into the sheepfold and cast a veil over nature "in a nicely Christian manner"?

Enough was enough. While the group was still together, Schelling would write a poem as a response to Novalis's essay. It would be aimed at both Novalis and Schleiermacher, as a kind of parody, with a title—"Heinz Widerporst's Epicurean Confession of Faith"—that drew on the eponymous character in a *Spruchgedicht* (spoken poem) by the Nuremberg Meistersinger Hans Sachs. Widerporst would personify the vices of obstinacy and recalcitrance.

Schelling's Widerporst presented a naturalistic view of the world, and the more Novalis drifted in the opposite direction, namely, into the belief in a heavenly authority, the more exaggerated this view would become. It would be concrete and folksy. Widerporst would invoke raw sensuality—not quite to an Epicurean level, but that was not the point as far as Schelling was concerned, or, at least, not the only point; what mattered was hyperbole, parody, polemic.

In accordance with Sachs's historical model, the poem was written in the form of *Knittelvers*, a kind of doggerel verse that originated in the Middle Ages. Schelling had learned it from Goethe. During their discussions about the philosophy of nature, Goethe had mentioned that he had taken up his work on *Faust* again and pondered using a strict form of Hans Sachs's *Knittelvers* in a parodistic mode, to portray an earthy, true-to-life commitment to sensuality in addressing the bodily needs of thirst, hunger, and sexuality. And because he was mindful that the word *Knittel* bore a phonetic resemblance to *Knüppel* (cudgel), Schelling's only rule was that two consecutive verses had to rhyme, so as not to bludgeon the reader:

> *Up to faith's youthful strength nature elevates*
> *And, once again youthful, it re-creates*
> *One force, one beat of the pulse, one life resolute*
> *An interplay of pausing and pursuit.*

The group planned to spend the rest of the afternoon outdoors at the river. The weather was clear, the Saale swollen. It was time for some fresh air.

Rulers Without a Realm

THE FAMILY OF GLORIOUS OUTLAWS

His hands clasped behind his back, his upper body leaning forward, he shifted his weight from one leg to the other in an ongoing change of tempo, the movement emanating from his hips.

It would have been startling to see Goethe among the ice skaters going around and around on the Saale from sunrise to sunset. He looked solemn in his long cloak, three-cornered hat, and stiff braid, cutting an awkward figure as he wound his way through the crowd full of woolen caps, skimming past the foliage that was barely higher than the ice, ready at any moment to grab hold of the puck.

Here in Jena he could indulge in these kinds of activities. The plan that had brought him from Weimar in the early part of the year had worked out well. Having Schiller and Wilhelm nearby gave him new inspiration; his work on *Faust* was making good progress, as was the translation of Voltaire's *Mahomet* (Muhammad), which the duke had wanted Goethe to render in German, in the hope that staging this play, a piece of world literature, would invigorate the theater in Weimar and bring it to new heights. This was no easy task. In contrast

Friedrich Preller, *Skating at the Swan Lake Meadows*, 1824 (detail)

to Voltaire, Goethe regarded Muhammad not as a fanatic or fraudster, but as a creative genius. His translation would have to walk a fine line.

Goethe would get far more work done if he were not constantly besieged by requests. In Jena, as elsewhere, everyone was always seeking his advice about one matter or another. Writers and scholars revolved around him like satellites, as if he were their fixed star, their sun, until he grew dizzy from the unwanted attention. The situation became even more dire when a whole swarm of comets closed in on him, as had happened the previous month. He could no longer dodge that whole group, particularly Moses Mendelssohn's daughter, who had evidently also arrived in Jena a few weeks earlier. In his diary he opted not to mention the encounter with Dorothea: "Went for a walk around noon. The weather was again quite lovely."

And now he was being asked to judge whether two texts that were the subject of heated discussions in the circle—a speech by Novalis about the crumbled unity of Europe and the future of Christianity, and a lyrical parody of that speech by Schelling—ought to find publication in the *Athenaeum*, possibly even side by side. That, in any case, was what Wilhelm's brother proposed, since, Fritz had argued, controversy was a component of thinking and conflict and the very element that fueled all of life. Dorothea Veit seemed firmly opposed to running the pieces together. Wilhelm did not want to include the poem without adding explanatory notes, but Schelling took strong exception to this option. Tieck stayed out of the conflict; he tended to stand apart from the rest of the group and form his own judgments.

Because they were unable to reach consensus, he, Goethe, would have to adjudicate the matter. In cases of serious disagreement, he was invariably asked to mediate. He simply could not bear to listen to their ongoing choruses of "Long live Goethe."

As Christmas approached, the residents of Leutragasse 5 decided to offer one another gifts of poetry, which was all they could come up with in the current situation, and which was, besides, more than enough.

At least Gustel had returned from Dessau. It had been eight weeks since her departure from Jena, marking the first extended separation of mother and daughter. There had been many changes in her life. Her confirmation, scheduled for Easter, had already taken place in Dessau. Gustel had also moved ahead in her musical training, making it a particular shame that the family had had to break off contact with the family of the jurist Hufeland in the wake of the dispute about Schelling's philosophy of nature, which had boiled over in the pages of the *Allgemeine Literatur-Zeitung*. Hufeland was the newspaper's editor. Gries had always played the piano at his home and accompanied Hufeland's wife, Wilhelmine, when she sang. The Leutragasse group could no longer even engage in the usual small talk about fashion, formal dances, or family matters. They were more isolated than ever from the rest of society, and had to pay careful attention to what was said, and to whom.

One thing had not changed since Gustel's departure: Everyone in the house loved, pampered, and coddled her; no one could resist her endearing squint or the extraordinary charm of her fine intellect coupled with childlike curiosity.

On Christmas Eve, Schelling gave her a present of a little poem along with a green sash to wear around her waist. It almost seemed as though he was now courting this fourteen-year-old girl as well. The age difference between them was barely greater than that between him and her mother. He also gave Caroline a small gift of a couple of bracelets, in addition to some lines of poetry. These little trinkets were of great significance under the circumstances.

That Christmas Eve could be spent so peacefully on Leutragasse was due in large part to Goethe's having settled the dispute between Novalis and Schelling. It had not taken him long to make his ruling. To no one's surprise, it was a Solomonic judgment: Neither of the two contributions would be published in the *Athenaeum*. One atheism dispute in Jena had been quite enough. Fichte's dismissal that summer was too fresh in Goethe's mind.

People were relieved by this judgment, which sought to strike a balance. There was already plenty of hostility to the *Athenaeum*. It was surely wise for its contributors not to tear each other apart on top of everything else.

When the poems had been read and the little gifts handed out, there was a brief moment of silence. By now they were well established as the "family of glorious outlaws" that Fritz had presciently dubbed them when he and Dorothea still lived in Berlin. Fichte's arrival in Jena after an absence of five months, just one day after Schiller had left the city for Weimar, did nothing to change that. He had come only to sell the house and to collect his wife and son for the trip back to Berlin. Even so, he once again made the case for his new plans. He wanted to establish a journal, the *Kritisches Institut*. But the differences between Fichte and the group were too great: While Fichte envisioned a neatly structured organization, Fritz and Wilhelm could only work in an impulsive and fragmentary fashion. They had nothing against the *Kritisches Institut* per se, but they did think it better for Fichte to find different people to work with. Fritz and

Wilhelm regarded themselves as "republicans," and Fichte as a little "monarch." They were rulers all, rulers without a realm.

Some music—perhaps a piano—would not have been unwelcome. What was that Shakespeare passage that Tieck had recently quoted as the group sat around the fire? "The mind I sway by and the heart I bear / Shall never sag with doubt nor shake with fear." But no sooner had Fritz and Dorothea fully settled into life in Jena than it began to cloud over.

On December 31, 1799, at the Wittumspalais in Weimar, an amateur group gave a performance of August von Kotzebue's farce *The New Century* in the presence of Duchess Anna Amalia. Kotzebue himself acted in it. As though the earlier debates at court about the commencement of the new century were not enough, the play laid out the dispute all over again.

Wilhelmine, the daughter of a wealthy merchant named Werhof, has years ago promised a country squire, Schmalbauch, that she will answer his marriage proposal on the last day of the old century. Wilhelmine wishes to delay her answer by a year, and so she argues for 1801. Her father, meanwhile, expects repayment of a loan from Schmalbauch's father on the first day of the new century, so he quarrels with his daughter. Schmalbauch senior is torn: On the one hand, he hopes that his son will enter into a marriage that will fetch him enough money to settle the bill; on the other, a fortune teller has prophesied that he will die on the last day of the eighteenth century. What should be done?

In the end, no one cares, and the big festivities are postponed until the following year.

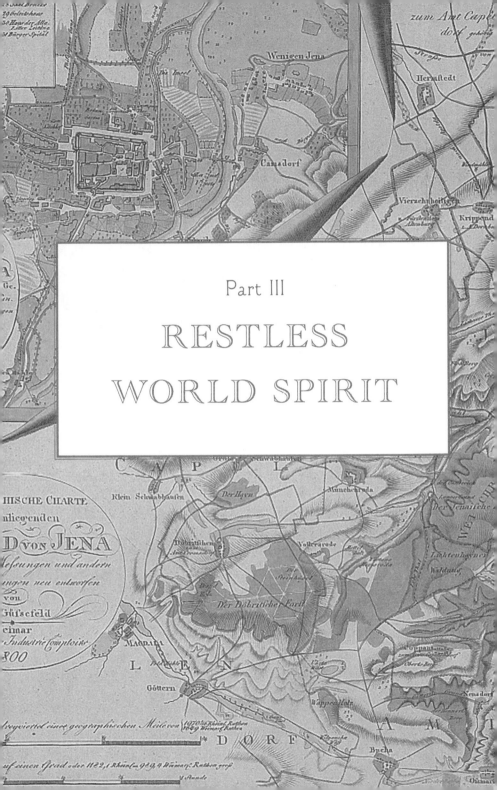

Part III

RESTLESS
WORLD SPIRIT

Gardeners and Scholars

SPECULATIONS OVER THE ABYSS

Fritz took to the lectern with nothing in his hands but a scrap of paper filled with mathematical symbols and all kinds of other scribbles. He employed this form of notation in his own notebooks, along with terse formulations and an array of recurrent ideas.

He rushed through his presentations and finished ahead of time. On one occasion—after closing a lecture with the words "Gentlemen, I will now briefly summarize the result of our deliberations: Devote yourselves to magic!"—he charged down from the lectern without looking where he was going, and banged into a pillar. The moment was anything but magical.

The students' reactions were split. Many were thrown by his nitpicking polemics and paradoxes. It might well be that a thousand ideas were brewing in his brilliant head, but in the audience's view, he lacked the ability to state them clearly. They were already used to some of these ideas from Schelling, but Schlegel's presentations went too far. What were they to make of the idea that the law of noncontradiction was not absolute, that in fact all of philosophy developed in an infinite series of contradictions? The logic did align with a particular form of thinking, but the source of truth, the genuine form, would need to be assessed at a higher level, which was why the first problem of philosophy, namely, determining the character of philosophy itself, could not be solved by pinning it down precisely, because that could only end up as a definition, and definitions, by definition, were dead. Try wrapping your head around that.

Fritz had no reputation to precede him; he struggled along as well as he could. No more than eighty people attended his inaugural lecture, far fewer than the numbers at Schiller's, Fichte's, or Schelling's. Schlegel's style was utterly different; he improvised. He had no need for or interest in neatly formulated manuscripts. No Schillerian poetic note, no Fichtean appeal at the end of the session, much less Schellingian pathos. There was nothing grandiloquent about Fritz. To him, philosophy derived life from experimentation, and anyone wanting to philosophize had to start afresh.

Only on occasion was Fritz able to get through to the students and set them on fire with his ideas. Then the auditorium would fill up for the next session, before the ranks thinned out again. He was unable to emerge fully from his role as a writer. He still needed to learn how to appear in public as an academic lecturer and teacher, even if he had already come up with his own reason for his mediocre success: His audiences were simply too stupid to absorb his sublime point of view.

Fritz announced that he would be offering two lecture series for the winter semester of 1800–1801: "Transcendental Philosophy," a private series, and "De officio philosophi" (On the Vocation of the Scholar), which would be offered to the public. The course fees for the private lecture series would keep him afloat for a time, although the compensation fell far short of the time and effort he was pouring into this work, particularly in view of all the money he'd spent on his doctorate. Dorothea hoped that they would recoup these expenses by St. Michael's Fair at the latest, if Fritz managed not to brush aside the whole thing in a fit of irony.

Meanwhile, Fritz had heard that Schelling had been hit hard by the sweet poison of melancholy. The two of them had yet to see each other since Schelling's return from Bad Bocklet, without Caroline.

Schelling played some part in the decision to go to a health resort in Lower Franconia. For quite some time he had intended to visit the hospital in nearby Bamberg, where two physicians, Adalbert Friedrich Marcus and Andreas Röschlaub, applied the method of the Scottish doctor John Brown more stringently than anyone else in Germany. This method, known as the Brunonian system, had been attracting attention throughout Europe for ten years. Brown claimed that illness was nothing but a deviation from the norm of nervous excitement. At one extreme, excitation was too high, at the other, too low. Health lay in a balance between stimuli and excitability, weakness and feverish physical exertion.

That spring, when Caroline suffered from a serious illness that required a long recovery—relapses kept sending her back to bed; at times her condition was critical, and the Brunonian system was the only treatment that helped—the time seemed right to combine two goals. Schelling promised Marcus and Röschlaub that, having taken a leave of absence from the university, he would offer a private lecture series on his philosophy of nature in Bamberg. Why not have Caroline go to Bad Bocklet to convalesce and continue her treatments, and he would stop over in Bamberg? Even Christoph Wilhelm Hufeland, an expert in the field of medicine and declared foe of the Brunonian method, supported the plan for his patient to stay at the health resort. Once Hufeland conceded that none of his therapeutic approaches were working, Schelling persuaded him to try out the method. He then administered quick stimulants and a steady stream of tonics to Caroline, along with Hungarian wine, nourishing creams, and strong bouillons. The wine, straight out of Goethe's collection, proved especially effective. As if by miracle, the patient suddenly improved.

Schelling had been weighing the possibility of leaving Jena for quite some time. Since Fritz had taken Wilhelm's side in the conflict over Caroline, his situation had become truly unbearable. A little distance, coupled with peace and quiet, would surely be good for all of them. He even asked Fichte whether he could see himself coming along instead of remaining in Berlin without any concrete prospects or solid livelihood. In Bamberg or Würzburg, they could accomplish more together. Although Bamberg was derided as a deeply Catholic two-bit town around which the Enlightenment had made a big detour—the city was known more for its vegetable gardeners than for its scholars—he wouldn't need to remain there. If all went well, Schelling could even relocate to Vienna the following year. He revealed these plans to Caroline.

On May 5, Caroline and Gustel set off, accompanied by Wilhelm. Schelling, who had departed two days earlier so that it would not look as though they were fleeing together, was waiting for them in Saalfeld. The sun was shining as though the harsh winter had never been. In bad weather Caroline would not have been permitted to leave her sickbed; she was still too weak on her feet. When he arrived in Saalfeld, Wilhelm silently handed over mother and daughter to his rival. His thoughts were already on the book fair in Leipzig.

Schelling had asked Dr. Marcus to find housing for them in Bamberg. For Caroline, the best option would be three simply furnished rooms, a living room, a bedroom for Caroline, and one for Gustel. Ideally, there would be an additional room to serve as maid's quarters—or, if need be, this space could be an alcove, a narrow spot for a bed next to the parlor. Schelling himself needed only a bright living room and a small bedroom, if possible all on one floor, or perhaps a garden house or other lodgings, as long as they were in a nice location. No matter how humbly Schelling presented his housing requirements, they were substantial. A hotel would not do, even on a temporary basis. It almost seemed as though he wanted to settle down permanently in Bamberg with Caroline and Auguste.

Fritz had greater success with the public lecture series, in which he attempted to counter the era's tendency to compartmentalize the arts and sciences and in so doing split up the grand intellectual community that actually bound them—philosophers, scholars, and artists—all together. No matter where you looked, there were intermediaries and interdependencies, and everything was in transition. Each made his contribution to the whole: The philosopher found the idea, the scholar developed it, the artist depicted it. They worked toward a single goal of reaching the infinite. The root of superstition, wickedness, and misfortune lay in restrictions, in an obsession with the merely finite.

Once Fritz passed his oral thesis defense in August, he was granted his doctorate on the basis of his studies of the literature of antiquity. Now that the final issue of the *Athenaeum* had been published, he could actually picture himself becoming a professor. Up until this point, he had refused to listen whenever

Wilhelm brought up that option. The career path of an academic appointed by the state did not mesh well with a freelance
writer's life. But his plan to earn a living by writing was proving
more difficult to put into practice than he had anticipated.

After delivering a sample lecture in mid-October, "On Enthusiasm," Fritz received his official authorization to teach. The
entire faculty was present. The theory that Fritz developed went
right to the heart of his thinking. Poetic and philosophical casts
of mind, he argued, are not mutually exclusive, but rather inter-
mesh in a state of enthusiasm. Plato had long ago declared, in
his *Ion*, that enthusiasm made it possible for us to embrace contrasts. Poetry and philosophy, in combination—not pure reason
alone—could lift the human mind up to a higher level, possibly
the highest of all levels: poetry by inviting the mind to experience the incisiveness of concepts, and philosophy by raising the
mind out of the stark boundedness of reflection via the elasticity
of figurative language. As long as people remained constrained
by conceptual thinking, they would be incapable of producing
poetry, just as people are incapable of deep thinking as long as
they are just wistfully dreaming through their days. This was
why Plato had the poets buzzing around like honeybees in the
gardens and glades of the muses; he saw poets as light, winged,
sacred creatures, unable to produce poetry until they have been
inspired and can lay aside pure reason.

Fritz presented a very different Plato from the political theorist who claimed that poets lied because—in stark contrast to
the philosophers—they were merely epigones, with no knowledge of the actual matter at hand. Schlegel's Plato understood
the power of the imagination and literature in shaping human
existence. He called enthusiasm a divine gift, a state of rapture
that served to open up people's eyes to the essentials, the dialogical simultaneity of poetic intoxication and philosophical

sobriety, and Schlegel took up this line of thinking. A person could only be transported or thrust into such a state, rather than bringing it about herself. To Schlegel, there were fundamentally inexplicable elements of divine inspiration, revelation, creative derangement, and, above all, love.

Schlegel agreed with his rival, Schelling, on many points. Just one year earlier, Schelling had published his *System of Transcendental Idealism,* the most complete account of his thinking to date, which also deemed art the crowning achievement of thought. For Schelling, aesthetic intuition was an unconscious activity of the mind that led to conflicts between freedom and mechanism, and he regarded it as the pinnacle, the keystone of all philosophy. Transcendental philosophy and the philosophy of nature were two sides of the same coin; the former ran from the *I* to nature, and the latter from nature to the *I.* Art ultimately reconciled the contrast between the self and nature by making the perceiving subject aware of the congruity of freedom, natural necessity, practice, and theory in an object of aesthetic intuition, namely, the work of art. In the medium of art, the mind could grasp its own consistency and inconsistency; past and future became transparent at the moment of unwitting artistic production. Art was the only true organ and document of philosophy.

But while Schelling tried to combine all parts of his philosophy into a single system, Schlegel insisted that each system had to have the capacity to keep destabilizing itself, or else it would become stale and abstract, a lifeless mechanism. Philosophy must always offer room for enthusiasm and skepticism. A non-system was just as indispensable for the mind as a system; the two must be linked dialectically and also subject to unlinking. Enthusiasm and skepticism were the driving forces that advanced philosophy step by step, little by little, epoch by epoch, toward their culmination. To Schlegel, the poetic mode was more a way of life than a form of knowledge, and required daily training; the life of the mind, he thought, was fulfilled in art, but in stark contrast to Schelling, he did not consider art its crowning glory. It was the work of many, in an ongoing back-and-forth, rather than the product of a single subject rising up to become the symbol of the human species as a whole at the moment of aesthetic intuition.

In his lecture series, Fritz did not buzz about in the manner of Plato's bees. Graceful restraint was advisable for someone wishing to advance in academia. And that was what he intended to do. Fritz was determined to outperform Schelling.

The Bocklet mineral springs had a long history. In 1720, a pastor named Johann Georg Schöppner had discovered a spring on the site while taking a walk, and he used his own money to have it dug up and encased. Since then, spa guests had flocked to the mineral-rich water.

After a full month, which Caroline and Auguste initially spent in Bamberg because accommodations for guests in Bad Bocklet were undergoing renovations, they arrived at the spa proper. Shortly thereafter, something happened that no one would have anticipated: While Caroline kept improving, and seemed to be almost fully cured, Auguste unexpectedly fell ill. Her situation appeared dire. The diagnosis was dysentery.

Schelling had just come back from a trip to visit his parents. His brother Gottlieb, a lieutenant serving in the imperial army, had been killed in action outside Genoa at the tender age of twenty-two. Austria was trying to drive the French out of Italy. They succeeded in Genoa, but just ten days later, at the Battle of Marengo, farther to the north, they suffered a decisive defeat. Before Caroline and Auguste left for Bad Bocklet, Schelling went to Schorndorf, a small town near Stuttgart, to be with his parents during this difficult time. It was a condolence visit; he had not been close to his brother.

When Schelling came back to Bad Bocklet, he found that Caroline was cured but Auguste was confined to a sickbed. He was alarmed by what he saw: She was pale, limp, and feverish, even though she had so recently accompanied Caroline and Schelling on excursions to the French gardens in Bamberg and had gotten to know Röschlaub and Marcus and members of the city's high society, bursting with energy all the while.

Despite her condition, Schelling radiated confidence that Gustel would recover. He recommended treatment with the Brunonian system of medicine, supplemented by opium. The doctors in Bad Bocklet concurred. What had worked for the mother would surely help the daughter.

On October 1, two years to the day after he had left Dresden to start a new life, Schelling was once again on the road, now heading out of Bamberg to Jena, knowing full well that nothing would ever be the same. Just one day earlier he had visited the small village churchyard in Bad Bocklet with Caroline and laid fresh flowers at her daughter's grave. The site offered a panoramic view of the whole tightly enclosed valley and the nondescript spa resort. The grave was kept simple; the tombstone provided the needed dignity.

Schelling looked back on the events of the previous months in bewilderment. First Caroline was severely ill, and then Auguste, of all people. How could a girl die in the prime of her youth? He blamed himself for failing to do everything in his power to ward off the danger in time. The most happy-go-lucky of all human beings had lost her life at a place where life and health sprang up right out of the ground.

Schelling and Caroline remained in Bamberg as long as they could, to get their affairs in order. Wilhelm came, as did Hufeland, and Gries also offered his condolences in person. The news of Auguste's sudden death spread swiftly. Everyone who knew her was shocked. Time was passing far too quickly; if only it could be slowed down.

Then the endless waiting in the coach began, just as it had before, with a village seeming to spring up from the ground at random every couple of miles. The roads were in wretched condition. There were potholes and mud puddles requiring reckless maneuvers; the stagecoach did not even reach walking speed, and could not get as far as twenty-five miles a day. Once again, Schelling was with Gries, with whom he had struck up a friendship back when everything had seemed so carefree. Exhausted, but unable to sleep, they tried to read in silence. Time melted into an indefinable clump in this brief, gloomy eternity as they listened to the clattering of the wheels, the rhythm of the hooves.

Schelling decided to scrap his Vienna plans for the time being. He was needed in Jena. Fritz, who was known primarily in the field of literary theory, announced that in the winter semester he would be offering lectures on transcendental philosophy. Transcendental philosophy was clearly Schelling's turf, so this came across as an affront. Schelling could not allow this dilettante, with his endless effusiveness, to destroy the solid foundation he and Fichte had laid. Schelling had always been put off by the "irony in the Schlegel family." Philosophy was not supposed to culminate in irony; it needed to come together as a system. Freedom and necessity intertwined, and philosophy had to supply the evidence. Like mathematics, it needed to proceed in a structured manner.

No trace remained of the enthusiasm or spirit of optimism he had felt back when he and Gries had finally arrived in Jena in 1798 after a journey made difficult by the terrible weather and sodden roads. They had alit from their coach as the town hall clock rang out its twelve chimes across the market square. He looked up instinctively to the tower, where, with each strike of the clock, a strange figure opened its mouth wide to snatch at a golden sphere that a pilgrim dangled from a rod, while an angel on the other side rang a little bell.

He hurried through the city in the very first hour of his arrival, intent on seeing Schiller. All around him were the sounds of moving wheels, of grunting and cackling livestock. When he finally met up with Schiller, just where they had last said their goodbyes and expressed hopes of reuniting soon with Goethe in his garden house right at the Leutra, their new beginning showed early signs of success. They found themselves switching into a broad and homey Swabian dialect as they discussed natural science and Goethe's theory of colors, with the whole afternoon ahead of them. The revolution could begin.

Now the whole thing seemed almost silly to him, like a dream. When the town of Saalfeld appeared before them out of the densely wooded landscape, he could hardly believe that such idyllic areas still existed. Schelling had lost something precious in Bamberg. If he was not careful, he would lose it all. He had to defend his place at the lectern.

Leaden Times

SCHELLING UNDER FIRE

Caroline was exhausted and ill. She and Wilhelm had traveled from Bamberg to Braunschweig to stay with her sister, Luise Wiedemann. They planned to spend the winter there, to get away for a while. Auguste's death had taken a toll. She had lost her daughter, her little gem, her everything, the center of her life. And she would have to carry on this existence as long as heaven allowed. All she wished for was peace and quiet.

She was well aware of Schelling's state of mind. His letters brimmed with profound melancholy. The depth of his suffering came nowhere near hers, of course, but in contrast to him, she had awakened from her lethargy, her leaden fatigue. As a mother, she continued to feel Auguste's presence at her side, saw Auguste before her when she closed her eyes, leaping through the room in flowing dresses and braided hair. Not for a moment did her beloved child depart from her, as long as Auguste was in her thoughts, whereas Schelling, abandoned by everyone, was drawn deeper and deeper into the maelstrom of divine sorrow.

It was a hard time. She suddenly had to take care of Schelling before seeing to herself, and there was no question of Schelling being able to take care of her, a mother who had just lost her child.

Caroline felt responsible for him. He needed someone to prop him up, someone whose encouragement would restore his self-confidence.

In this situation, Goethe became Caroline's last hope. She was convinced that no one else could save Schelling. A good word, a nod, from the privy councilor would do the trick; a little show of interest was all that was needed.

She knew that in the fall, Goethe had devoted considerable effort to studying Schelling's system of transcendental idealism, line by line. He had spent an entire month in daily colloquia with Niethammer, finding his way into Schelling's way of thinking and unlocking its major mysteries.

Caroline asked—begged—Goethe to lure Schelling out of his punishing isolation. If he still had hopes for Schelling, if he cared about Schelling at all and what he had achieved to date in the field of philosophy, he would understand her sense of urgency.

With each passing day the *Allgemeine Literatur-Zeitung* continued to fire up readers' emotions. Founded in 1785 by the Weimar merchant Friedrich Justin Bertuch and edited by the classical scholar Christian Gottfried Schütz, the jurist Gottlieb Heinrich Hufeland, and the writer Christoph Martin Wieland, the publication had quickly become one of the leading German review journals, and within a single month, the number of subscribers exceeded one thousand. The editorial staff felt obliged to promote Kantian philosophy. Some even claimed that without the journal's support, Kant's *Critique of Pure Reason* would have landed straight in the wastepaper basket.

The journal had power, and it now trained this power on attacking Schelling, using the death of Auguste to wage a debate about the Brunonian system of medicine and the principles of the so-called philosophy of nature, which it regarded as nothing but a highly refined form of obscurantism, pure mystical enthusiasm, which made it all the more hazardous. It was one thing to have earned a doctorate at the university and to debate hypotheses; it was quite another to aim to "cure" people with idealism—and to wind up killing them.

The medical case of Auguste Böhmer had become a matter of public concern. On the one side were the proponents of a speculative philosophy of nature, on the other the defenders of a methodologically tried-and-true natural science oriented to Kantianism. In this conflict, which had been brewing for quite some time, the girl's death seemed almost beside the point.

Disputes from the previous fall were now revived as well. Schelling's idea of turning transcendental philosophy into a philosophy of nature had become a target of criticism. Two anonymous reviews were published in the *Allgemeine Literatur-Zeitung*, one by a physicist, the other by a philosopher, and both tore apart the *Ideas for a Philosophy of Nature*. Schelling's attempt to place a third, clarifying review by Henrik Steffens was flatly rejected by the diehard editors.

The tenor of the criticism had not changed in the slightest: Even though the methodology of the philosophy of nature might be ingenious in one respect or another, it was not rigorous—in other words, it was not scholarly.

This criticism ate away at Schelling without shaking his conviction. In fact, it reinforced his certitude that a new theory of knowledge, designed for a new century, could not be damaged by such immature articles. But it sapped his strength to have to defend himself against the constant attacks, to battle out the dispute by any journalistic means; he felt drained by the time evening fell and he was surrounded by quiet.

His former companions had broken off contact with him, and he could expect no support from them. His break with Fichte was definitive; Fichte still resented him for what had happened with the *Kritisches Institut.* Fritz and Dorothea had rented an apartment of their own. They also considered him partly to blame for Auguste's death. When Schelling returned, he found the house on Leutragasse deserted, an eerie silence having replaced the lively group debates. It was Wilhelm, of all people, who lent him support and defended him whenever he could. Wilhelm was not about to be thrust into the role of the jealous husband who had been robbed of his stepdaughter.

When Schelling was up to his neck in crisis and tormented by depression, he received a letter from Weimar. Goethe invited him to spend the year's end with him there, surrounded by friends. And someone else had gotten in touch with him. Schelling could hardly believe his eyes: his old friend Hegel, from their university days, announced that he would be coming. Even in those leaden times, he had sources of support after all.

It was the dawn of a new century in Weimar. Goethe, Schelling, and Schiller stayed at home on Frauenplan. How uneventfully major events seem to unfold! Not even the corks popped with the proper wild abandon.

There had been plans for a big celebration; Schiller in particular had made the case to the duke for a major fête, a sort of Roman carnival featuring masked figures on the streets and squares, a folk festival with booths on the promenade, and an extraordinary carnival in the theater, with individual acts and scenes from the current repertoire offered on the stage and food on the ground floor. August Wilhelm Iffland, Germany's preeminent actor, could come to Weimar, as could the acclaimed Ferdinand Fleck, who had taken on the role of Wallenstein at the Hoftheater, along with some two hundred guests. A new era would await its arrival in style.

The plans met with widespread support, but the duke vetoed them, claiming that the political situation was too fraught, the community too riven for such a celebration, especially if it was being held in honor of a new century about which no judgment could yet be formed. The prospects were not rosy: Carl August feared riots, even in Weimar. Just recently there had been a duel over a trivial matter, involving a man dancing with a woman at the court ball. The times were that explosive. One of the duelists, a poet—and not a bad one—had sustained severe gashes on his left calf, and almost bled to death. It would take someone well versed in fencing to explain how the épée had managed to inflict such damage. Then there was the smoldering conflict between Kotzebue and his followers on the one side and the Schlegel circle on the other, which could easily escalate into a major confrontation. And there was the financial cost of a grand fête. Christian Gottlob Voigt, the executive officer who had been wondering whether the paltry state coffers could possibly suffice to host two hundred guests, breathed a sigh of relief. In turbulent times, a solemn, low-key ceremony was far more appropriate than a raucous party.

Even on December 26, at the masquerade ball at the Alte Casse, the converted town hall in the market square, there was little evidence of a festive atmosphere. Caroline had asked Goethe to invite Schelling over for the Christmas holidays and New Year's Eve, and so Schelling and Steffens traveled to Weimar together. Schiller was there as well. Tipsy from champagne, Goethe chattered away unselfconsciously, downright jauntily, while Schiller grew more and more serious and held forth in long monologues on aesthetic questions. Goethe tried to distract him with constant needling. Steffens stayed remarkably sober. Schelling observed these goings-on from his chair in the corner while raising a quiet toast to Goethe.

Just as Steffens was preparing to say good night and leave for Jena, Hufeland joined them. The jurist needed some time to orient himself in the room, since he could see with only his left eye. There was no forgetting the unlucky incident that had brought on this partial blindness: After spending a total of three hours on the road in cold, wet weather in an open carriage to see a patient, he had come back drenched and freezing. Goethe's *Hermann and Dorothea* lay on the table. Hufeland picked up the book and eagerly read it through to the end by candlelight, until midnight. When he awoke the next morning, his right eye was blind; he saw nothing but dark gray clouds. Even he, as a physician, could find no explanation for what had happened. Hufeland had to restrict his activities and interrupt his studies of pathology, but he was ultimately undeterred and resumed his work. After turning down multiple invitations from the Russian tsar, preferring instead to stay with the duke and the University of Jena, he had now received a letter of appointment from Berlin to become the Prussian king's personal physician and director of the Charité hospital.

Hufeland was keenly aware of the increasingly tense atmosphere in Jena. The French Revolution, the Jacobinism that was burgeoning everywhere, the recently ubiquitous singing of the Marseillaise . . . Mistrust had taken hold among monarchs and rulers. This was also true of the duke in Weimar, who came to Jena far less often, particularly after Fichte had to leave the university. Carl August made no further mention of the urgently needed hospital that Hufeland had been promised when he was appointed. There was widespread malaise at the university as well; people were wary about the future. The case involving Fichte spoke volumes.

Because the throne in Prussia was occupied by Friedrich Wilhelm III, who did not hesitate to enact domestic political reforms, and because the prospects in Jena had grown dimmer, Hufeland now wanted to seize the opportunity to work in a major hospital and lead a less confined life in the more liberal society of a big city.

For Schelling, it felt like a betrayal that someone like Hufeland, who was an institution in Jena and Weimar, would go to Berlin: first Fichte, now Hufeland. Maybe Andreas Röschlaub, from Bamberg, might become Hufeland's successor; if not, the student population in Jena would dwindle once again.

Goethe, Schelling, and Schiller did not stay up late on New Year's Eve. Shortly after midnight the little group split up. Schiller did not have far to go to get to Windischengasse, and Schelling would stay over at Goethe's place. On the program for the New Year's Day concert was Haydn's *Creation*.

There were big celebrations in Braunschweig on this special New Year's Eve, but Caroline and Wilhelm decided to stay at home. They were in no mood for festivities and high spirits. Luise briefly slipped out to a ball, but she was back by ten o'clock to look after her sister.

The death of Auguste brought Caroline and Wilhelm closer again, but the discord of the last two years could not be set aside. Wilhelm noticed that Caroline's mind was always on Schelling. She spent every morning waiting for the mail to arrive, and counted the quarter hours until it was there.

Caroline had sent Schelling a British overcoat at Christmastime. It was not intended as a Christmas present, but simply to keep him warm, even though the first few times he wore it, it kept shedding fur and his other clothes had to be brushed again and again. Still, it was comfortable, and freed up his arms to hug his girlfriend while he wore it. Schelling gave her a ring with his name finely engraved on the inside.

As New Year's Eve wore on, Wilhelm, who was feeling unwell, dozed off on the sofa in the upstairs parlor. He almost slept through the beginning of the new century, which, after all those discussions, was finally set to launch.

When the clock struck twelve, he was jolted awake. Caroline, who, with her sister, had prepared an apple punch with cinnamon liqueur, was just coming up the stairs. The clock was still chiming in the parlor. Wilhelm went toward her. They stopped halfway up the staircase and exchanged a glance, but nothing was left of what they had been to each other. Their estrangement was now entering a new century. From outside the window, they could hear the old night watchman strike up his song.

Hegel and the Nutcrackers

PHILOSOPHY IS NOT FOR MINDLESS MUNCHING

Schelling was overjoyed to reunite with his old friend Hegel, who was now planning to stay in Jena for an extended period. The two had roomed with Friedrich Hölderlin at the Tübinger Stift seminary, and they invoked grand words when it was time to say goodbye, speaking of the "kingdom of God" and the "invisible church on earth" as they sang the praises of freedom and reason.

Famous names were associated with the Stift, most notably Philipp Nicodemus Frischlin, Johannes Kepler, and Friedrich Christoph Oetinger. Hölderlin, Hegel, and Schelling had sworn that one day their names would also shine brightly in the ranks of the alumni.

Hölderlin and Hegel, both born in 1770, enrolled at the university when they were eighteen and lived at the Stift. Schelling, who was born in 1775, arrived two years later. He was gifted—extraordinarily so—and endowed with the self-assurance of a minor god. His heroes were Plato, Herder, and Kant. When the faculty at the Latin School in Nürtingen realized that there was nothing left to teach him that he had not long since taught himself, and the Bebenhausen Abbey school's instructional wellsprings had also run dry, he was given special authorization, at the age of fifteen, to study in Tübingen.

All three of them chose theology as their field of study so as to become respectable members of society. Their fathers would have loved to see them become pastors or teachers—certainly not philosophers or poets. But it soon became evident that these parental wishes would likely come to naught.

Together, Hölderlin, Hegel, and Schelling watched the ascent first of Kantian and then of Fichtean philosophy, and they celebrated this ascent just as frenetically as they had welcomed the spirit of the French Revolution. They read French newspapers, and devoured every news item that arrived. Hegel in particular was more interested in the politics of the day—the events in France—than in theological sophistry.

Their focus ranged far beyond the kind of political freedom, or freedom from dogmatic coercion, that could be achieved overnight. In a more comprehensive sense, they regarded freedom as an unending process of liberating the human species as such, as an ongoing challenge to existing constraints and boundaries, including those that were self-imposed. A new era seemed to be dawning. If the light of day had come up with Kant, it was now shining so brightly with Fichte that the mists would soon disperse altogether. This profound hope, shared by the three roommates, kept them going as they faced the dreary daily routine at the Stift.

The University of Tübingen, one of the oldest in Europe, was a training center for educational and ecclesiastical work. The duchy of Württemberg also boasted the Karlsschule, in the city of Stuttgart, which was attended primarily by doctors and lawyers.

In comparison with Stuttgart, Tübingen seemed to belong to an earlier time. The streets were narrow, crooked, poorly paved, and barely illuminated in the evening. There were dung heaps in front of the buildings on many streets. For a city that called itself the second capital and seat of government and boasted a famous university and a regional court, these were intolerable conditions. The contrast stood out all the more because Tübingen was located in a region with an exceptionally beautiful landscape, right at the Neckar River, surrounded by meadows, vineyards, and orchards. Southwest of the city, close to the Swabian Alb, Hohenzollern Castle towered above, the ancestral home of the Prussian kings, though it had been occupied by French troops since the War of the Austrian Succession fifty years earlier.

Life at the Stift was guided by Swabian pietism. Residents were expected to be devout, hardworking, and humble, and live by the Stift regulations that had been enforced since 1752. The daily routine was unvarying: rise at six in the morning, hear Latin sermons, and read psalms, all without breakfast. Then came three class periods, and lunch at eleven. Sermons were delivered during the communal meals, each about ten minutes long. Each man was required to take his turn at holding these sermons, for which he was rewarded with an additional portion of food. Recess followed, lasting until two o'clock. In town, the residents of the Stift were also known as the Blacks on account of their strict—and strictly monitored—attire. Cloak, collar, buckled shoes: all other ornamentation was forbidden.

In the afternoon there was church, as well as lessons and lectures, and, on Mondays, the weekly exam administered by an advanced student. After dinner at six o'clock there was a second recess, which lasted until curfew. Woe unto those who were not back by then. Ensconced in their rooms, they engaged in disputes, enjoyed tobacco, and played card games. Student assistants, attendants, and servants moved about stealthily, spying in the hallways, trying to root out something forbidden that they could report to their bosses, the directors of the Stift, anything that might earn them a favorable glance.

Kantian philosophy burst into this dreary routine with a vengeance. Its message—interpreted as an attack on the standard scholarly preachings—held out one major promise: freedom. On long evenings the *Critique of Pure Reason* was studied as a group, page by page.

Only Hegel was underwhelmed by it. Kantian theory struck him as dry terminological quibbling. In Tübingen he was known for his Swabian stodginess. He came across as staid and old before his time; he loved to sit quietly and enjoy a beer, a glass of wine, or a tarot card game in preference to engaging in more active pursuits. His friends appreciated his sociable nature, but when it came to dancing or fencing, Hegel was hopelessly clumsy, slow, and stiff. His fellow students drew caricatures of him as an elderly man making his way down the street bent over a cane. He was less taken with Kant than with Jean-Jacques Rousseau; he was fascinated by Rousseau's idea of a state that expressed not merely the *volonté de tous*, the sum of all individual wills, but rather the *volonté générale*, the general will of all people.

But orthodoxy and dogmatism were not about to be overturned so easily. In Swabia, the Enlightenment continued to be tolerated only in the terms put forth by Christian Wolff, that is, in a strictly rationalistic sense. Anyone who spoke out in protest, wanting more, had no choice but to go abroad—just as the most celebrated Swabian to date, Friedrich Schiller, had been forced to learn a decade earlier.

The will to disobedience was in clear evidence, however. One bright spring Sunday morning, Hegel and Schelling went out with several friends and planted a liberty tree on a large meadow just outside the city, like the Jacobins in Paris. *Vive la liberté!* Their actions came to light, but the duke in Stuttgart

Il retourne chez ses égaux.

Discours sur l'égalité des Conditions.

Illustration for Jean-Jacques Rousseau's *Discourse on the Origin and Basis of Inequality Among Men*; copperplate engraving by Nicolas de Launay after Jean-Michel Moreau, 1778

showed leniency and went no further than rebuking the "spirit of insubordination" their behavior demonstrated. In 1793, when Hegel completed his studies, he had to make a decision. With Schiller's help, Gotthold Stäudlin, a mutual friend from Stuttgart, sought to get Hegel the post of house tutor with Charlotte von Kalb in Waltershausen, near Meiningen. At the same time, he received an offer from Bern. Because the political conditions in Switzerland had captured his interest, Hegel opted for Bern. Hölderlin took the job in Waltershausen in his place. He wanted to be part of Fichte's closest entourage in nearby Jena, and to join in with this group. Hölderlin often wrote to Schelling, who was preparing to take his examination in theology, and had already published his first book—*On the Possibility of an Absolute Form of Philosophy*—which attracted even Fichte's attention, and he kept in touch with Hegel. Soon Hölderlin was sharing a little garden house outside the city with fellow student Isaac von Sinclair, and he spent whole evenings in discussions with Fichte and Novalis (who was also attending the lectures on the doctrine of scientific knowledge) about religion and revelation and about all that lay ahead for philosophy, a field of inquiry that was far from finished.

In May 1795, Hölderlin left the city in haste, fearing he had disappointed Schiller, who, along with Fichte, was one of his two major role models. He spoke to no one about what had happened.

Hölderlin went to Frankfurt, where he soon ran into Hegel, who had also applied for a tutoring job there. Schelling had now taken a position with the Riedesel family as a tutor, first in Stuttgart, then in Leipzig, publishing one work after another, before taking a giant leap to Jena, with Goethe's support. Meeting up with his old friend Hegel again in Frankfurt brought back memories of how it had felt to join forces with others against the rest of the world.

The plan to which Hölderlin, Hegel, and Schelling devoted themselves in Tübingen was radical. They were convinced that the revolution in thought proclaimed by Kant needed to be carried to completion by means of a second revolution, directed at the world and at life, in a reversal that would lead the way out of the divisiveness of the current age. Kant himself had spoken of his philosophy as a revolution, because it would allow the field of metaphysics to catch up with the revolution in ways of thinking that had long since become the scientific standard in the field of physics. Just as physicists had come to realize that reason understands only what it has itself fashioned according to its own design, there needed to be a realization in the field of metaphysics that our perception of things is limited to what we ourselves read into them. That objects are constructed according to our perception of them and not the other way around, that we cannot learn anything about the things in themselves—that was the fundamental revolutionary idea that Kant used to shed light on metaphysics, which had hitherto blundered about in the darkness of mere speculation.

Kant had given the word *Wissenschaft* (the pursuit of knowledge) a new meaning. There were general and necessary principles underlying all knowledge a priori, that is, even before any experience. On the side of understanding, there were twelve categories, among them the principle of causality, which David Hume had already relegated to the realm of mere habit; on the side of sensuality there were the two forms of intuition—space and time. For Hume, the fact that the sun would rise in the morning was at best a certainty in light of human experience, but not something that could be substantiated intellectually, whereas Kant's examination of the human mind demonstrated that there were ineluctable principles underlying any experience. Kant contradicted Hume by showing that objectively valid knowledge was possible. But in Tübingen they were not content with a simple reform of *Wissenschaft* of the sort Kant had initiated. Kant's revolution created a counterrevolution, with the crucial distinction that the counterrevolution was really understood to be a continuation of the revolution.

The problem that Hölderlin, Hegel, and Schelling identified in Kant, and that would henceforth set a precedent for them under the rubric of premises and results that followed the spirit but not the letter of a philosopher's thinking, centered on the dilemma that the forms of our cognition, which provided a basis for all possible knowledge, were themselves in need of a basis. Kant had postulated one, but he did not derive it in any strict sense. Although the human mind needed to acknowledge its own limitations, each limitation had been established at some point; none could be considered primal. The boundaries of critical philosophy were merely subjective: over there was the world of phenomena, and over there was the world of the things themselves. To get beyond the boundaries set by Kant, one needed to get behind them. It appeared as though Hölderlin, Hegel, and Schelling had set their sights on an incomparably more radical revolution in thinking, one that would aim at getting to the very origin of all knowledge—with Kant, yet beyond Kant.

One man who came to their aid from a conceptual point of view was Friedrich Heinrich Jacobi, a philosopher from Düsseldorf who resided at Pempelfort, his country mansion in Westphalia. A full generation older than the threesome, he was in contact with the best-known people of his day: Johann Gottfried Herder, Gotthold Ephraim Lessing, Johann Georg Hamann, Moses Mendelssohn, and Goethe. Jacobi, who described himself as the "privileged heretic of idealism," entered the public eye in 1785 with his book *On the Teachings of Spinoza, in Letters to Herr Moses Mendelssohn.* In writing about Baruch de Spinoza, he had chosen to devote himself to the study of a philosopher whom no one was reading anymore, and whom many regarded as a "dead dog." Spinoza's motto was *Deus sive natura* (God or nature), with no difference marked between the two—God and the real world merged. He was the absolute substance, and anyone who recognized the relationship of things to one another grasped the essence of God. All was necessary, determined, and ascertainable by means of cognition. Spinoza insisted that there was no place for a god as creator, in any religion, a heretical doctrine for which he was banished from the Jewish community in Amsterdam in the middle of the previous century.

But the key point of Jacobi's brief book on Spinoza was his claim that in July 1780, a good half year before Lessing's death, Lessing had become an adherent of Spinoza. Emotions ran high in the Enlightenment salons in Berlin: Spinoza's doctrine amounted to fatalism, nihilism, atheism. Anyone who joined sides with Spinoza was undoubtedly an atheist himself. And were they to think that Lessing, of all people, had done so? His legacy was in jeopardy.

Mendelssohn mounted a sweeping defense of his friend, and called the book he wrote on this subject, which took a stand against Jacobi, *Morning Hours, or Lectures Concerning the Existence of God.* The allegation of atheism in particular could not go unquestioned. Anything that cast Lessing in a bad light would also discredit the circle of the Berlin adherents of the Enlightenment, who had gathered around Mendelssohn. In his view, there could certainly be a "refined Spinozism" that was compatible with morality and religion, that could tie in with the existence of a god as creator.

The debate kept widening. Goethe and Herder sided whole-heartedly with Mendelssohn, yet the dispute about the published correspondence with Jacobi took an increasingly visible toll on Mendelssohn. Just a few days after bringing the manuscript of his work *To the Friends of Lessing* to the printing press, he died unexpectedly. Already in poor health, he had evidently caught a chill from going out in freezing weather without an overcoat. When Karl Philipp Moritz, Mendelssohn's protegé, also joined the debate in order to avenge Mendelssohn's death, the philosopher's daughter Dorothea intervened. Dorothea's earliest education had come from her father, and her hand had been promised to the banker Simon Veit at her father's wish. She urged Moritz to keep his composure; things were bad enough as they were.

Jacobi was enthralled by Spinoza's thinking right from the start, in particular by his *Ethics*, the substance of which Spinoza believed he could derive according to a strictly geometrical— that is, mathematical—method. But his fascination focused on one particular facet: Spinoza's statements were irrefutable, seeing as his conclusions were all logically correct. But was there truth to what Spinoza was saying simply *because* he did not contradict himself? Jacobi resolutely denied that idea. The truth was not enclosed like a nut in a shell just waiting for a thinker to crack it open. Philosophy was not for mindless munching.

For Jacobi, Spinozism was the negative foil he could use to develop his own thinking. He conceded that Spinoza was right to claim that the existence of God could be proved, but only to the extent that God was conceived as the essential nexus of all things. Salvaging the living God, the God of creation, would necessitate catapulting oneself out of the system, venturing a salto mortale, a leap into uncertainty.

Hölderlin, Hegel, and Schelling were not willing to be as dauntless as Jacobi, their great admiration for Spinoza notwithstanding. But they understood that if there were a system of philosophy—and Kant had also had this sort of systematic thinking in mind with his critique of reason—Spinoza had already developed it. Hölderlin, Hegel, and Schelling were transfixed by this degree of sophistication. They understood that Jacobi's dispute with Spinoza was also a criticism of Kant, of the openness and contradictory nature of his system, which fluctuated, chameleon-like, between idealism and realism, hovering indeterminately in the middle. But in contrast to Jacobi, they believed that Spinoza's thinking—if related not to the divine substance, but to the subject—held out the promise of freedom, the capability of striking out anew, on one's own, in a world saturated with determinism.

That was precisely what the Tübinger Stift students were after. They were driven by a longing for a grand comprehensive unity of all thinking and being that would lead out of the havoc of the present day. They sought the *hen kai pan* of Heraclitus, which, as they saw it, could be achieved only in human freedom.

Hen kai pan—one and all: Hölderlin wrote these words in Hegel's autograph book before the three friends went their separate ways. They swore that they would see one another again in the realm of freedom.

When Hegel arrived in Jena in 1801, there was not a hint of the "old man" about him, none of the sluggishness he had displayed in the past, even though what had prompted him to switch over to the academic sphere after all these years was the death of his father. He and his brother and sister divided the assets among them. All of a sudden they had come into an unexpectedly large sum of money. Money meant independence, and the gift of the time he needed to complete his studies. What flashed through his mind was Jena, where Schelling, his old Stift compatriot, was teaching.

Even after Fichte's departure, Jena remained a mecca for philosophers. The course catalog was bursting with offerings in the field, running the gamut from the dogmatism of antiquity to the latest philosophy of nature. The competition was intense. Each philosopher had his own system, and followers eager to hold it up as the only true philosophy. Friedrich Schlegel, editor of the controversial *Athenaeum*, which had recently been discontinued owing to a lack of subscribers, had also been giving lectures in the field as of late.

Hegel had been following Schelling's ascent from a distance. He now faced Schelling with a feeling approaching reverence. But Hegel also wanted to get in on the act and create his own system to surpass his friend's, even though he did not plan to show his hand for the time being. Schelling was looking forward to their upcoming conversations, especially now that so many people in his life had turned their backs on him, Caroline was in Braunschweig with her sister, and he had to stand up to Fritz. The pair's original project, which they had thought up together in Tübingen, remained just as timely.

Once Hegel arrived in Jena, he headed straight into the fray. All of thirty-one when he got there, he had already lost too much time; Schelling had been named associate professor by the time he was twenty-three. To enhance his image and stake out his own territory, Hegel now worked on a treatise setting out the difference between Fichte's and Schelling's systems of philosophy.

At the same time, he embarked on a project about the orbits of the planets, which he planned to use for his postdoctoral thesis. This study of the philosophy of nature, in large part a concession to Schelling, aimed not only at providing ingenious proof of a rationale behind planetary motions but also at carrying forward the analysis of Johannes Kepler, an alumnus of the Tübinger Stift and a fellow Swabian.

Hegel, like Kepler, embraced the ancient Platonic notion of a *harmonia mundi*, a harmony of the world that could be grasped by means of reason. Kepler, not Newton, he argued, was the first to formulate the elliptical form of planetary motion, even though, strictly speaking, he was not the first to deduce it. In order to school himself in these matters, Hegel studied every last one of the famous mathematicians, physicists, philosophers, and astronomers. Plato's *Timaeus* had already specified a numerical series according to which the demiurge, the first among the craftsmen and creators, had given form to the universe: 1, 2, 3, 4, 9, 16, 27. Everything could be deduced from this sort of series: the orbits of the planets, the trajectories of the comets, the distance between the constellations . . . The universe could be measured without any need for a telescope.

Hegel was yet another Swabian to arrive in Jena, following in the footsteps of Schiller, Paulus, Niethammer, and Schelling. It seemed as though everyone in Swabia wanted to emigrate in order to restore the university in this third century of its existence. Soon people were saying that Schelling had brought from Swabia to Jena an avid supporter who would make it plain that Fichte's time had run out. It was a minefield, but one that needed to be explored.

Hegel also attended Friedrich Schlegel's lectures on transcendental philosophy. In early February, when the lectures had already been running for more than three months, he joined the audience just in time to hear the pivotal concluding section of the "return of philosophy into itself," in which Schlegel explained why all philosophy had to be dialectical and not purely logical.

Hegel found lodgings at the home of Johann Dietrich Klippstein, who worked in the Botanical Gardens and ran a small nursery near the city limit. Johann Diederich Gries, Schelling's close friend and associate, lived right next door, which would prove handy in getting settled in. There was a chance that Hegel would move in with Schelling, and there were even plans for them to publish a journal together. The relationship between Goethe and Schiller was of a very different sort, but even so, the union of Schelling and Hegel was regarded as the new dream team.

Kant in Fifteen Minutes

When the famous French writer arrived in Berlin in early March 1804, the city was in the midst of preparations for Queen Luise's birthday ball. She was welcomed as a guest of honor; people were flattered by her presence.

Once in Berlin, Germaine de Staël—commonly known as Madame de Staël—never passed up an opportunity to quench her insatiable thirst for knowledge, for German philosophy, and for poetry. Over dinner she asked to have Fichte's philosophical writings explained to her, in a way that she could use a short time later to surprise the philosopher himself. Fichte could barely follow her half-baked remarks, fired off in fast-paced French, concerning the opposition of the *I* and the world, and how to mediate between these poles in practical terms. She was on a constant quest for new material for her book, which continued to expand in length and scope. Fichte, frightened off by so much exuberance, did his best to explain transcendental philosophy in fifteen minutes, though fifteen years would not have sufficed. Madame didn't really care, anyway.

Driven out of Paris by Napoleon, she set off on a trip through Germany to gather material for her book, to be called *De l'Allemagne*, that would serve as a bridge between French and German culture. She was fascinated by this inaccessible land, its philosophy and its poetry, about which nothing was known in France.

The writer Benjamin Constant, with whom she shared a daughter and a fraught relationship (it was said that he was not the only man in her life), had awakened this love in her, and shown her that German literature could no longer be the object of scorn. German philosophy in particular, she decided, was more refined, evenhanded, and precise—and clearly more truthful, bold, and temperate—than French and British philosophy. Since reading Goethe's *Werther*, initially in French translation, and deeming it one of the most important novels in modern literature, along with Rousseau's *Julie, or the New Heloise*, she decided that the French language and literature, and the nation itself, were too confining. She wanted to write about all the insights she had amassed: about the country's customs, and where the Germans were still lacking in this area; German literature, which stood out well above that of all other nations; and philosophy, which was then in full bloom.

Immanuel Kant, to whom this land was so indebted, had died just a month earlier in faraway Königsberg, shortly before his eightieth birthday. He had never left his hometown, yet he was the most widely discussed author in Europe, as a philosopher who had not become outdated even at the end of his life, in spite of his advanced age, and whose relevance would not diminish for a long time even after his death. Kant was the very embodiment of the boundary between two epochs in philosophy.

The indomitable de Staël gained a deeper feeling of what she was missing as she studied German philosophy, namely, a place to settle down and regain her equilibrium. She was filled with gratitude to learn the existence of some singular words in German once she finally mastered the language: *Heimweh* (homesickness), for instance, which expressed a painful, nearly insatiable longing to return to untrodden territory. She experienced *Heimweh* wherever she was received in Germany, in spite of all the affection she was shown, in spite of all the festivities, formal dinners, banquets, and balls in her honor.

Madame de Staël and her entourage headed to the Musenhof in Weimar. She had intended to remain for two weeks, but wound up extending her stay to two and a half months. She was warmly received by the duke, and greeted in person by Goethe, who had once sent her an edition of his novel *Wilhelm Meister*; she hadn't fully appreciated the gift at the time, in part because of her insufficient command of the language, but now the situation was altogether different. Everyone was talking about her latest book, *On Literature in Its Relations to Social Institutions and the Spirit of the Age*. No one had ever taken the approach of investigating how literary works were shaped by the specific environment in which they originated. Society, climate, geography, everything had to be considered.

There was nothing that did not interest Madame. She spoke quickly, and Goethe, like Fichte, had to pay close attention so as not to lose the thread of the conversation as she jumped back and forth. In Weimar, she also met with Böttiger, that incessant blabbermouth, who was resolutely pursuing but making no headway on his project of constructing a literary monument for Goethe. He had been following de Staël's literary ambitions for years. As it turned out, back in 1797, shortly after the German translation was published, he had read her book *On the Influence of Passions on the Happiness of Whole Nations and of Individuals* and discussed it with Wilhelm Schlegel. Goethe suggested that

Louis Le Coeur, *Coronation of Napoleon*, Paris, December 16, 1804

for help with her new book project, she might contact Schlegel, the professor who had so often been helpful to him in matters of style, metrics, and literary translation, but who had moved to the Prussian capital three years earlier to lecture on literature and the arts.

When de Staël left the city for Berlin, Goethe was glad that he had not gotten more deeply involved with her. He was exhausted from being bogged down in conversations every chance she got, when he knew full well that these conversations would be mercilessly exploited for literary purposes. Böttiger got on his nerves for the same reason. After de Staël's departure, he felt as though he had suffered through a long and difficult illness.

Once the initial fuss died down—half of Berlin paid her a courtesy visit, including princes, dukes, and diplomats—de Staël finally got to do what she had come for: attend August Wilhelm Schlegel's lectures.

Goethe had not overstated his praise of Schlegel, who had moved to Berlin from Jena in 1801 and had been divorced from Caroline since 1803. The professor was precisely how she had imagined him: smart, entertaining, and charming. He was not a handsome man, at least not in her view, but he didn't have to be; she knew right off that he would be the ideal colleague and companion for all occasions. No one knew his way around literature, intellectual matters, and scholarship better than this man; he spoke French like a Frenchman, and English like an Englishman, and there was hardly anything he had not read.

De Staël did not hesitate for a moment, and tried whatever she could to persuade Wilhelm to come with her on her travels. Ultimately, she decided that he was too distinguished to educate her children; she needed him for herself. There could be no better adviser for her book than Wilhelm, an invaluable asset for her educational journey through Europe, a walking encyclopedia, a genuine souvenir.

No sooner had she presented this offer to him than she learned that her father, who was staying at Coppet Castle on Lake Geneva, was severely ill. Dark premonitions haunted her. First her fatherland, now her father.

That very day she decided to go, earlier than she had planned. Wilhelm had to make a quick decision—and he said yes. What was there to hold him back? He had been divorced for a year, he was deep in debt, and de Staël was offering him a generous salary. But his motivation in leaving with her was not purely financial; it was also a desire to open up a new chapter in his life, to leave everything behind—both academic teaching and his unhappy, ongoing love affair with Sophie Bernhardi, the sister of Ludwig Tieck, who was not entirely innocent in the case of his disastrous financial straits—and to launch into a promising future at the side of a celebrated writer. De Staël envisioned establishing in Geneva a new, cosmopolitan, liberal, unpretentious Republic of Letters, taking up the tradition of the Paris salons when Diderot, Hemsterhuis, D'Alembert, Buffon, and Melchior gathered together. A supernatural power emanated from her, and there was no fighting it off. Once again, Wilhelm was poised to place his fate in the hands of another person, but he felt that at long last he had found what he was seeking.

Wilhelm left the Prussian capital with de Staël on April 19, 1804. In Weimar they would meet up with Benjamin Constant, who could give them news about her father's state of health. They also planned to stop in Würzburg, where Schelling and Caroline were now living.

When he got into the coach and watched the shadows of the linden trees go by, it almost felt like a final farewell, as though

Wilhelm would never again see Berlin, or any of these surroundings.

Caroline could hardly believe it. For perhaps the first time in her
life, she felt that this would be forever. Dorothea Caroline Al-
bertine, née Michaelis, widow of Böhmer, divorced from Schlegel, had remarried again, and was now the wife of Schelling. She
was determined to stick with this name—and she did.

Her wedding to Schelling was attended by only the closest
family members. In late May 1803—just days after her divorce
from Wilhelm—they had come here, to Murrhardt in Württemberg, where one month later they were joined in marriage
by Schelling's father, Friedrich Joseph Schelling, the newly appointed prelate. On the way to Swabia they stopped at the country churchyard in Bad Bocklet for Gustel's blessing.

Divorcing Wilhelm was no easy matter for Caroline, but both
knew they were standing in the way of their own happiness and
that of their spouse. They had never been right for each other,
and Wilhelm knew it, even though he had always stood by her.
It was impossible for them to give each other unconditional love
and devotion. By now they had gone back to using the formal
Sie in their correspondence. Still, their friendship would endure.

Caroline and Wilhelm wanted the divorce to proceed as
quickly as possible, regardless of what others might say. They
sought to do what they thought was right, but they needed the
consent of the duke, and that was difficult to obtain, as there
were neither legal nor moral grounds for terminating the marriage. Luckily for them, a different case came to their aid, one
that the consistory had recently adjudicated with a positive out-
come. Sophie Mereau had separated from Friedrich Ernst Carl,

a Jena law professor, after meeting Clemens Brentano, the young medical student who had skipped his early morning dissections of corpses, preferring to pursue his literary inclinations, attend Caroline's lunch gatherings, and visit Frau Mereau in the afternoons while her husband was lecturing. This affair had important legal consequences: At some point, both Mereau and Carl wanted a divorce, which was ultimately granted, thereby creating a legal precedent that might facilitate the proceedings in which Wilhelm and Caroline now found themselves. At least, so they hoped.

It was no easy matter. Herder was on the panel, in his capacity as chief clergyman, along with Böttiger, who represented the school authorities. Wilhelm was not on the best of terms with either of them. He had always kept his distance from that pesky Böttiger. Herder was of a different caliber. Wilhelm and Fritz owed a great deal to some of his writings, such as his treatise on the origin of language, but in the *Athenaeum* they had shown little regard for him, and had ridiculed him repeatedly, even though one of Herder's ideas—that the language of sensations did not stand in opposition to the language of reason—served as a guiding principle for their idea of a poetry that moved between the extremes.

Customarily, the consistory summoned the two spouses to take stock of the situation in a conversational setting, as a last chance to save the marriage. Herder and Böttiger insisted on setting up such a meeting. Caroline was told not to leave the city. It now seemed as though her final remaining option was to confide in Goethe, and sure enough, he was able to persuade Herder and Böttiger to come around. The meeting was canceled, and no scandal developed. The duke granted the petition for divorce, and once it was finalized on May 17, 1803, Caroline and Schelling made their way to his parents' home.

They wanted to spend the first few months of their marriage with Schelling's parents in Swabia. The war prevented them from journeying on to Italy, as they had planned. Caroline was welcome at the home of her in-laws. As a fellow theologian, Schelling senior knew Professor Michaelis, Caroline's father, and had even corresponded with him. Still, it was not easy for the Schellings to accept their son's choice of a wife who was twelve years older, divorced, and pardoned by the king. Sometimes the past simply had to be left behind in order to see how beautiful the future could be.

Out there at the borders, the war raged on.

Very few members of the group remained in Jena by the end of 1801. Tieck had long since departed for Dresden, Wilhelm had made a permanent move to Berlin in the winter to lecture on literature and the arts, and Fritz and Dorothea had moved to Paris. Novalis was out of the picture. The ranks had thinned, the dream had come to an end. The beautiful Tower of Babel lay in ruins.

As Schelling, who continued to share a bond with Hegel, compiled the pages for the first issue of the *Kritisches Journal der Philosophie*, he increasingly pondered the possibility of switching universities. Scholars were offered higher pay in Prussia, and Bavaria was about to reorganize its university and educational system; at the moment, anywhere else seemed like an improvement. It was feared that the sharp decrease in the number of students would preclude some courses from running. Following the example set by Napoleon, many rulers had decided to forbid their citizens from attending foreign universities. The situation was wretched. Even so, he and Hegel had now founded their journal, and the first issue would be printed before the end of the year.

Schelling and Hegel hoped that the *Kritisches Journal* would help stem the tide of the appallingly unphilosophical doctrine that was being preached on the pulpits in Jena and written up in countless magazines. The *Allgemeine Literatur-Zeitung* continued to set the tone for the charges of insanity being leveled at the Jena Circle in its entirety, charges that drew no distinctions between Fritz, Wilhelm, Schelling, and Hegel. Fichte, meanwhile, was now presenting suggestions to the group about setting up the *Kritisches Institut*, to be run by Fritz, Wilhelm, Schelling, and Fichte himself. Fichte planned to line up a staff of fourteen editors.

Schelling and Hegel decided at the outset to issue the *Kritisches Journal der Philosophie* as a joint undertaking. No sideshows, no machinations. Cohesion would be the guiding principle.

They co-authored the programmatic opening essay, "On the Nature of Philosophical Critique in General, and Its Relationship to the State of Contemporary Philosophy in Particular"; sharing authorship, too, was a first. Schelling and Hegel wrote most of the article together, and for the parts that were composed separately, they did not consider it necessary to indicate who wrote what. Each gave and received as he was able, and the main ideas took shape in conversations, little by little. Afterward, they would not even be able to tell who had actually written what. Whereas Fritz and Wilhelm always made a point of indicating the authorship of each contribution in the *Athenaeum*, Schelling and Hegel appeared as a single philosophical entity. They shared the conviction that independence of spirit was vital, and they had no intention of forgoing controversy to achieve a glib, vapid unanimity. In contrast to Fritz and Wilhelm, however, they were not radical individualists; indeed, they warned against fragmentation, and sought a consistent, supraindividual system. Just as only a single pursuit might be rightfully called reason, philosophy too, in terms of its claim to validity, could be only a single pursuit. Strictly speaking, there could not be different views of a true plurality, as all views lay within the one and only framework of reason.

Schelling and Hegel also held this view in regard to philosophical critiques. Critiques, they insisted, were neither a matter of taking sides nor expressions of subjective claims to power or opinions. The two of them thought of their purpose as a quest to unveil the ideas within things, to distinguish philosophy from non-philosophy in such a manner that the latter, in the ongoing progression of thinking, would turn out to be philosophy after all. Polemics were not ruled out—Schelling and Hegel made ample use of them when necessary—but they were not meant to become the rule. The task of philosophical critiques was to refute an opponent's arguments in a cogent manner.

The language of the two former theology students had also undergone a fundamental transformation. The passion with which they once conjured up the kingdom of God or the invisible church on earth yielded to a cool, muted tone; in some spots the texts were even interspersed with formulas, mathematical and otherwise. They now spoke of identity and difference in regard to the absolute, form and essence, production and product, and quantitative indifference. The book that Hegel had recently published, *The Difference Between Fichte's and Schelling's System of Philosophy*, even addressed the question of "identity of identity and non-identity," a totality of reason that contained within it both itself and its opposite. (Hardly anyone understood what he meant by that.)

Hegel presented the idea of a "speculative Good Friday." God was dead, he argued, and because he no longer held his hand protectively over humankind, everything had to be engulfed in the obscurity of bewilderment and doubt. Everything came back to the beginning, Hegel wrote, and thinking commenced at the point of nothingness. When thinking finally turned to self-observation, it discovered that nothingness was not in fact nothing, but the beginning of something that took on an increasingly concrete form by means of reason in the succession of its operations, whereby reason, too, was both nascent and in constant motion. To Hegel, reason was not an instrument that people could maneuver as they wished, but a living organism that produced and developed on its own.

At first Hegel was interested only in adopting a polemical, critical standpoint to show that contradictions surfaced in all forms of finite knowledge, so he raised doubts about everything and proceeded with an utter lack of presuppositions, but it turned out that this skeptical process could be transformed into a positive method. Thinking that had entered the process of reflection recaptured the poles between which it oscillated in the course of its own movement. He did not intend this dialectical model to express something new; he was merely trying to get to the heart of what Schelling had envisioned in his concept of an absolute system of identity. Nothing was given other than by reason itself, in Hegel's formation, and nothing eluded the realm of its conveyance. Schelling was impressed.

In late 1801, the *Kritisches Journal der Philosophie* went to press. Their work on the first issue already made it clear that Hegel had a mind of his own, and would not be swayed to suit Schelling's purposes. In some matters his thinking was actually far more radical than Schelling's, since his philosophy was even more starkly conceptual, which he deemed the manner of true philosophical speculation. He had now completed his postdoctoral degree as well, and was holding lectures on logic and metaphysics. There was no scandal attached to his post-doctoral certification, as there had been for Fritz that spring. Even Goethe had already expressed an interest in the new man in Jena. Natural science was not exactly in Hegel's wheelhouse, but Goethe had to concede his admiration for the way Hegel tried to develop Kepler's laws of planetary motion a priori in his postdoctoral dissertation.

The pieces in the *Kritisches Journal* were published under both of their names, but Schelling had to take care that his former roommate did not work his way up to becoming the leading philosopher of the new century. At the beginning of the new year, the first copies would be sent to subscribers—and thus into the world at large.

Clearing New Ground

IN THE MINE OF POETRY

On March 19, 1801, the fourth anniversary of his young fiancée Sophie's death, Novalis's health went into a rapid decline. He felt drained, and sensed that he had only a few more days to live. He needed to hold out now that Fritz had announced he would be coming to Weißenfels. Novalis would have loved to have been present when his friend was granted his postdoctoral degree.

Novalis's health had been deteriorating since the late summer of the previous year, when he began to suffer severe abdominal pains and relentless pressure on his chest, and found blood on his handkerchief. This came after a fine start to the year 1800: his engagement to Julie von Charpentier, daughter of the Saxon mines inspector Johann Friedrich Wilhelm von Charpentier. His new father-in-law, who had friendly ties to Goethe, gave him advice in all matters pertaining to the mines in Ilmenau and—like Abraham Gottlob Werner, with whom Novalis was still in close contact—taught at the Freiberg University of Mining and Technology, where he himself had studied.

Novalis's personal and professional prospects at the time could hardly have been better. He had been working as a mining official in Weißenfels, some twenty miles south of Halle, and had already been promoted to the post of saltworks assessor. Now he was about to be appointed district administrator for the electorate of Saxony. In addition, he was working on the continuation of *Heinrich von Ofterdingen*, his response to *Wilhelm Meister*, which incorporated what he saw as the missing piece in Goethe's work—nature, the mystical element. The first part had brought him admiration, and the prospect of an encyclopedic project that could fill an entire library. But these promising visions and plans came to an abrupt halt with the onset of illness in August. Work was out of the question. When he received word in November that his brother Bernhard, age fourteen, had drowned in an accident at the Saale River, Novalis suffered a severe hemorrhage that nearly cost him his life.

The winter took a severe toll. His mind and body sluggish, he was a shadow of his former self. His brother Karl and his fiancée, Julie, hovered over him constantly, doing their best to take care of him. Seldom did he join in discussions; he simply listened or even fell asleep while the others conversed. He lay there like a dead man, yet when his chest rose and fell, he still seemed so alive.

In mid-February he was examined by a Professor Stark, the same doctor who had treated Sophie. Stark, too, was at a loss to come up with a treatment plan, and the physicians deemed Novalis a lost cause. Even so, he seemed oddly relaxed, almost jovial, perhaps precisely because no one could help him and he was now on his own. The philosopher, the "transcendental doctor," had always known best how to restore a damaged, feeble body to a state of equilibrium by means of a gradual augmentation of internal stimuli, thus boosting and nurturing the body's own sensitivity. The tragic death of Auguste Böhmer had done nothing to diminish Novalis's enthusiasm for the Brunonian system of medicine. His fear was gone, along with his daily struggles. It was just a matter of not losing heart or faith, which would mean losing everything. Prayer was a panacea.

Sometimes he was able to write a poem. He also spent a great deal of time reading the Bible, religious works, Zinzendorf, and Lavater. He was also taken with the writings of Jakob Böhme. The mystic and theosopher sparked ideas for linking philosophy and religion. Perhaps there was a way of saving something like a "religion within the bounds of bare reason," as Kant had titled one of his books. Novalis now had a better understanding of Socrates's decision to portray philosophy as a form of training for dying. A person needed to learn how to die before he actually died, needed to be prepared to yield to the destiny that certainly awaited.

For a short time, Novalis believed he was recovering; the blood, the cough had vanished without a trace. He felt a bit weak, that was all. Maybe things would eventually turn out, and he would become not just the prophet of a medicine of a higher self, but the fulfiller of said prophecy. In his *Blütenstaub (Pollen)*, a collection of philosophical fragments that was published in the *Athenaeum*, he had written that eternity—its worlds, past and future—was nowhere to be found but within ourselves: "We dream of traveling through the universe, but isn't the universe within us?" Once his health improved, the world at large would discover what poetry could truly be, with all the splendid poems and songs now constantly buzzing around in his head. The mission was far from over.

That night, Fritz would be getting together with Dorothea, Paulus, and a couple of the other former *Athenaeum* associates for a congratulatory feast in his old residence on Leutragasse. Dorothea had organized the evening for him.

She had flourished since they moved to their new home. Now that Caroline was no longer setting the tone, Dorothea felt liberated, and like she had been pushed around by Caroline for far too long. Fortunately, Caroline and Wilhelm were not yet back from Braunschweig, and the rear building was deserted. It was the ideal place to celebrate Fritz's newly obtained postgraduate degree, the next step on the academic career ladder, though the process had almost ended in a major scandal.

Procedural disputes had surfaced before the defense even got under way. As a rule, postdoctoral degree candidates were entitled to designate their own challengers for the oral defense, yet in Fritz's case the practice was suddenly altered. The authorized examiners rummaged through the files, blew the dust off the book covers, and fished out an ancient law stating that it was incumbent solely upon the faculty to determine the challengers. They insisted on adhering to this law. And that was that.

The faculty selected as challengers Johann Christian Wilhelm Augusti and Johann Friedrich Ernst Kirsten, both openly hostile to the *Athenaeum* circle. Fritz saw this move as a clear provocation; obstacles were being placed in his way. But because he was reluctant to cause trouble in advance, he refrained from standing up to this harassment. On March 14, 1801, when the disputation began, he seemed calm and even-tempered.

The test lecture in the fall on the Platonic concept of enthusiasm had gone so well that Fritz once again chose Plato as his theme. He spoke about Plato's approach to philosophy, which meshed with his own explanations and outlook. Although Plato had a philosophy, he had no need for a system; his philosophy could endure only as a thought process in motion, of the kind Socrates drew on as he walked about in the marketplace and put the opinions of the Athenians to the test. Plato's thinking never reached an end; he always tried to use conversations to depict his striving for complete knowledge and insight into what was behind it all, this perpetual process of becoming, shaping and reshaping his ideas. Fritz was equally disinclined ever to be finished with thinking, or with philosophy, or with life itself. All of philosophy was more a quest, an eternal striving for knowledge, than it was a corpus of settled knowledge.

For this reason, he continued to be wary of his colleague Schelling's systematic approach. You could *become* a philosopher, he thought, but never actually *be* one; as soon as a person thought he was a philosopher, he stopped becoming one. Fritz had retained much of his earlier delight in irony, but he no longer invoked it as a method, as it had lost its relevance for the points he was making.

Starting with Plato's understanding of idealism, Fritz proceeded to map out his own concept of philosophy to the faculty, discussing the relationship between idealism and realism, morality and politics, art and science, the role of poetry and the imagination, and the value of mythology and history. Fritz basically regarded his philosophy as the only true idealism, because it was the only form that did not operate in strict correlations, but instead retained the fragmentary and provisional open-endedness that was required for thinking. His announcement the previous winter semester that he would offer a lecture series on transcendental philosophy was thus an eccentric means of taunting Schelling.

All went well at first, but when it came to the final challenger, Augusti, a theologian, scandal erupted. Augusti seemed to make a habit of weaving snide remarks into his arguments. Fritz bit his tongue at first, but eventually these remarks so grated on his nerves that Fritz cut him off, crying *Tace, tace* (be silent, be silent). This was precisely the situation he had always feared, the reason he had long ago decided not to take up the profession of an academic instructor, but rather to earn his living as a free-lance writer, to stay independent.

Augusti took up the perceived challenge, kept up his taunt-ing, and eventually quoted a passage from *Lucinde*, which he referred to as the *tractum eroticum Lucinda*. No sooner had Fritz heard the word *Lucinda* than he interrupted Augusti once again, hurling the word *Scurram!* (fool, fraud) while ranting and raving about what wretched subservience was being demanded here, what a miserable, rundown operation was this academy. The dean admonished him to be quiet, to let his challenger say his piece, and to wait and find out the reason Augusti was quot-ing this passage. When he added that, in thirty years, there had not been a scandal of this sort on the philosophical stage, Fritz retorted, in the finest academic Latin, that there had been no such *iniustitia* (injustice) for the past thirty years either. The few supporters he still had were eventually able to calm him down.

Fritz had absolutely no regrets when he proposed a toast that evening on Leutragasse. He might have crossed a line in insult-ing his challenger, but he would do it again. He'd had to bor-row money for the examination, as he had for the doctoral exam the previous fall. This time he received the needed loan from his well-heeled friend Brentano, but he and Dorothea remained con-fident that at some point they would be able to make ends meet.

But a different matter weighed on Fritz's mind. His old friend Novalis, whom he had known for close to ten years, lay on his deathbed. The doctors had evidently given up. The di-agnosis was unequivocal: tuberculosis. Some suspected that he had caught it from Schiller, whom he had visited often even during Schiller's worst flare-ups. As soon as the excitement about his postdoctoral degree died down, Fritz intended to go to Weißenfels, wishing once again to see Novalis, who had always felt like a kindred spirit.

Fritz and Novalis had met in 1792, when the two of them came to Leipzig to study law and Novalis's name was still Friedrich von Hardenberg. Their fathers both wanted them to become civil servants.

While Fritz had already begun a business apprenticeship in Leipzig—a position he would soon abandon—Novalis studied law in Jena, or at least pretended to. In reality he attended lectures by Schiller, primarily on the philosophy of history, and during Schiller's illness built up a close and intense rapport with the writer. After two semesters, his father, Heinrich Ulrich Erasmus von Hardenberg, who had been the manager of the salt mines of the electorate of Saxony in Artern, Kösen, and Dürrenberg since 1784, realized that a disaster was looming. Hardenberg *père* had a talk with Novalis's former tutor, Carl Christian Erhard Schmid, a colleague of Schiller, asking him to arrange for a private discussion in which Schiller might urge the young Hardenberg to pursue his legal studies and prepare in earnest for his future life in business, for his own good and the good of the family. A word from Schiller, Hardenberg explained, would accomplish more than endless fatherly reprimands.

By the time Novalis moved from Jena to Leipzig, he had written literary texts, including poems attesting to his dedication to and feelings of friendship for August Wilhelm Schlegel, who had already made a name for himself as a philologist and literary critic. Novalis had yet to establish personal contact with him. When Friedrich, Schlegel's brother, suddenly stood before

Novalis, he sensed the beginning of an act of divine providence that would grant him access to a circle of kindred spirits who would accord him the recognition that had eluded him thus far. Novalis poured out his heart to Friedrich, telling him about his previous studies, about Schiller, and about Jena while speaking three times more quickly than usual, and ended up presenting the poems to him, asking for his opinion, and requesting that they be passed along to his brother if at all possible.

Fritz took on the unexpected role of critic. He liked the young Hardenberg. He looked through the texts and saw, beyond their many shortcomings—the unrefined nature of the language; the choppy meter; the digressions that invariably stopped short of their aim; the opulent, embryonic images, which seemed as though they originated in the transition Ovid described from chaos to the world as we know it—the potential for a great poet: originality, acuity, and receptivity to all shades of perception. People could listen to Novalis all night long and never tire of following along with his ideas; his vision could transform even the most commonplace objects into poetry. This young man could turn out to be everything—or, for that matter, nothing.

Novalis and Fritz did not intend to submit to the fate predetermined by their parents. They were fascinated by art, philosophy, and religion. But while Fritz was discovering the role of the freelance writer for himself, first in Dresden and then in Berlin, and pursuing this uncertain path alongside his brother, Wilhelm—who was immersing himself more and more deeply in ancient and modern European literature and philosophy (he had long since put aside his studies in Leipzig)—Novalis essentially acquiesced to his parentally designated role, and in early 1796 became the assessor at the local salt mine administration in Weißenfels.

In the end, he found a way to combine his poetic work with his humdrum obligations. This, too, was something he had

Ore mining in Freiberg, Saxony; copper engraving, 1820 (detail)

learned from Schiller in Jena. A contradiction was actually a productive thorn in the flesh that posed a challenge to surmount the contrasts. On the one side was what Schiller called the *Brotgelehrter* (bread scholar), who works solely for material and professional advancement and forfeits any delight in thinking per se; on the other was the *Universalgelehrter* (polymath), who is distinguished by the ability to absorb these very contradictions and eventually rise above them.

Novalis took up a second course of study in the natural sciences with Professor Werner at the Freiberg University of Mining and Technology. Philosophy and natural science could be studied in tandem there, and he could also acquire the requisite knowledge for work in the management of salt mines. That was precisely what was meant by Fritz's phrase "progressive universal poetry": *Poiesis*, in its original Greek meaning of "make" or "generate." To "produce" creatively was not a literary process, but a way of life that needed to be practiced every day, even if the issue at hand was mining coal.

From then on, writing was only a secondary matter to Novalis. The main issue was always the mechanics of everyday life, and everyday life never focused exclusively on any one thing. Writing functioned as a means of education, a way of pondering and processing with care, but a complete education required having been a tutor, a professor, a craftsman, *and* a poet. Hardenberg now went by the name "Novalis," derived from an ancient family surname based on the Latin phrase *de novali*, meaning "clearer of new ground."

Soon he was leading a study group to research and chart coal deposits to the south of Leipzig. In Jena, he met with Fritz and Wilhelm at the Döderlein House. Their aim was to poeticize even the most ordinary life, a life full of the most mundane interests. Poeticizing, they insisted, was nothing but qualitative potentiation that brought the baser self, tainted as it was with all manner of mundane adversities, into accordance with a better, absolute self. Poeticization occured by investing lowly matters with a higher meaning, lending the commonplace a transcendent touch, and giving the finite the sheen of infinity. By the same token, the higher, unfamiliar, mystical, and infinite took on a commonplace aspect, turning accessible, present, sometimes even menacing events, like an illness, into essentially the mere expression of a higher emotional connection.

When Fritz left Jena in late March 1801, he hoped that Novalis's poeticizing would be borne out.

Although Novalis's health was declining markedly, the two friends were able to enjoy each other's company when Fritz finally arrived in Weißenfels. They exchanged views, brought each other up to date on the news, and talked about their work and their plans, with little breaks here and there.

Two days later, Novalis, now significantly weaker, looked up something early in the morning, but by breakfast time he was tired out again. From his sickbed he asked his brother Karl to play the piano. Novalis laid the book aside, the way he used to do when he finished reading books so quickly that everyone thought he had just leafed through them. Then he fell asleep, while in the background the music played on.

Novalis had fallen into a slumber from which he would not awaken. Toward noon, Fritz, Karl, and Julie noted his passing. His breath—the final one—had died away without the slightest sign of pain, as though once and for all his mind had triumphed over his vexatious life and found its way to a new, gentler existence.

The Night Before

The news about the end of the Holy Roman Empire of the German Nation had spread like wildfire in the summer. No one was really taken by surprise. For quite some time, the empire had been no more than a plaything in the hands of Napoleon. Franz II had abdicated and had himself crowned Emperor of Austria—as Franz I—once Napoleon made it clear that he would never wear the imperial crown. Even so, the French invasion had not been expected; it had come overnight. French soldiers were right there on the Jena town square.

Hegel, who had stayed in the city, had his hands full on the morning of October 13, 1806. Six men showed up at his apartment and searched the rooms, and when they found no money, they took clothing, linens, and copper jars. Hegel catered to them as well as he could, getting them bread, eggs, sausage, and brandy. He had no choice but to offer them a feast.

Hegel had a premonition of the developments that lay ahead. He had concluded his course of lectures on logic and metaphysics at the end of the summer semester by commenting that mankind was at a crossroads, in the midst of an upheaval. The mind had experienced a jolt and was about to alter its form; the bulk of previous notions, the traditional order of the world, had dissolved and fallen away like visions in a dream. Philosophy was set to welcome a new phase of the mind, because the eternal nature of reason was manifested in it; nothing would be more disastrous at that historic moment than to cling to the past. With these words, Hegel dismissed his students for the semester break. He did not know how right he would prove to be.

Over the course of the weeks that followed, more and more new battalions were stationed in and around Jena and Auerstedt. Prussia was mobilizing. One hundred thirty thousand Prussians and twenty thousand Saxons marched toward the French army. Napoleon had dared to offer the British the electorate of Hanover, which Prussia had just received earlier that year in exchange for the political and military neutrality of Prussia in the Battle of Austerlitz, which Napoleon had won in December, exactly one year after the imperial coronation. But who would have thought that Jena would get caught in the crossfire? Forty years of peace following the Seven Years' War had given the city an air of imperturbable insouciance. The Prussian leadership would surely be clever enough to relocate the scene to the left side of the Rhine if battles should ensue. No matter what, the Prussian cavalry seemed utterly indestructible, as steadfast as the spirit of Frederick the Great.

Even Hegel could never have imagined that an upheaval of great significance to world history would take place there in that university town in Thuringia, right in front of his eyes. He had had no concept of this sort of breathtaking swiftness; no one had, not even those who had been watching the events up close. It was only when the news of the death of the prince arrived on October 11, 1806, that the sense of security in Jena finally evaporated. Prince Louis Ferdinand of Prussia, commander of the Prussian vanguard, had been killed in a battle at Saalfeld, and the nine thousand soldiers with him were driven out. War was looming.

At some point Hegel found the house too chaotic. Suitcases, boxes, closets had been pried open. The more securely something was locked up, the greater the likelihood that something valuable might be hidden in it. A chair lay in the corner, its cushions slit open, and the floor was littered with paper, pens, and knives; nothing had remained in place. Clean and dirty laundry, bread, scraps of food. The bedlam was absolute.

When Caroline returned to Jena from Braunschweig in April 1801, she stayed at the Döderlein House on Leutragasse. Her hope, that she might be able to rent the garden house where she had stayed when she first came to Jena with Wilhelm, had been dashed.

Reluctantly, she stepped into the old residence. Fritz and Dorothea had left the house in wretched shape. Caroline heard that during the previous month they had celebrated Fritz's postdoctoral degree here, in the parlor where her portrait still hung. Given the state of the house now, it must have been a boisterous gathering.

Caroline shuddered at the thought of staying in this hovel any longer than absolutely necessary. But the lease ran for one more year, and there was little likelihood of affording the rent for a second apartment at the same time.

Wilhelm had left Braunschweig for Berlin, where he hoped to give lectures on literature and art. He had several translation projects—of Shakespeare and Calderón—lined up as well, and he had finally found a publisher for this work. It almost seemed to

Caroline that a divorce would give both Wilhelm and her a new lease on life.

Hegel tucked under his arm the papers that did not fit into his satchel as he left his apartment at the old fencing hall next to the Red Tower. These were the final sheets of the manuscript he had just completed. The previous week he had already sent most of the manuscript to the publisher in Bamberg. He could only hope that it had found its way. The very thought that even one part could get lost was unbearable; he would hardly know how to replace any of its pages, nor could he imagine losing out on the remuneration he was entitled to. He had decided on the title: *The Phenomenology of Spirit.* It was planned as an epic work that would eclipse everything that philosophy had produced to date. He left the rest of his books and papers to their fate. Hegel had with him all that he needed.

He was fleeing to the home of Carl Friedrich Ernst Frommann, the publisher. Frommann's austere-looking house, situated behind a high, inconspicuous entrance gate on Fürstengraben, was one of the few properties to be spared from the lootings. The lady of the house, Johanna, had displayed admirable prudence and levelheadedness when the first Frenchmen came through the city with their torches. The courtyard gate was bolted, the shutters facing onto the street fastened, the blinds lowered in the rooms.

When the regular troops arrived, though, they revealed their presence and opened up the house for billeting. As many as eight officers camped out with their staff in the publishing house, setting up an entire riding stable in the back. Together with all those from Jena who, like Hegel, had sought refuge here, there were up to 130 people camped on beds and straw.

Hegel saw the emperor on his way to Frommann's home. Napoleon's imminent arrival had been announced at the noon hour. Many people supposed that one marshal or the other actually *was* the emperor. Those who thought they had already seen him did not know him, and those who *did* know him had yet to see him. Hegel, standing there in his slippers—his boots had been pulled right off his feet—was now a witness to the world soul and its entourage riding through the city gates. This was the future of Europe, concentrated in one spot. That is precisely what world souls do: They permeate the world, from its innermost core right through to the outermost periphery, creating an organic relationship between the whole and its parts—even the least important ones; microcosm and macrocosm, from earth to heaven and back.

The way Hegel saw it, Napoleon Bonaparte was less the military genius, hero of Austerlitz, and ruler of the continent of Europe than the great crafter of the civic code, the Code Napoléon, civil law organized according to revolutionary ideals in what may have been the most significant body of legislation in recent history. It would be impossible not to admire him for that.

For the time being, Frommann was safe from lootings and other such menaces. The generals, officers, and soldiers appreciated the courtesy they were shown at the publishing house and kept their sabers drawn and rifles at the ready to frighten off invading mobs. Hegel would be able to stay there for the next few days.

Toward the end of 1801, Fritz and Dorothea left Jena for good. Their destination was Paris, the old capital of philosophy and the capital of a new world. Caroline and Wilhelm had moved to

Jena little more than two years earlier, yet those years felt like an eternity.

Paris held out promise for Fritz and Dorothea, not because they loved the city so much or sought to promote cultural exchange between the Germans and French, but because it offered the best opportunities for a freelance writer—a free spirit like Fritz—to earn a living. The air in Germany rendered people submissive.

Fritz recalled the example of Georg Forster, who, after the shortlived revolution in Mainz, had found many ways to make money from writing while in the French capital. In Germany everything was forcibly suppressed, while Paris was open-minded, cosmopolitan, and synthetic in every direction—*and* it was the artistic repository of Europe. The Napoleonic robber barons brought their loot here from all over the world. No other European city had more art on display and more significant names to scrutinize. By comparison, the picture gallery in Dresden looked like a measly storage room.

In the spring, shortly before France and the Holy Roman Empire signed a peace treaty in Lunéville and thus ended the War of the Second Coalition, the novel on which Dorothea had been working all those years, bearing the title *Florentin*, was finally published—anonymously, of course. As to whether the second part of *Lucinde*, on which Fritz had been working for an eternity, would see publication, Dorothea had stopped believing that day would ever come. *In Jene life is bene*—those times were long gone.

Certainly no one in Jena had pictured the war this way. Anyone who had not witnessed a war had no concept of it; equally in the dark were those who thought that if they'd seen one war, they'd seen them all, because no war is like another. What did survival matter if you had to watch corpses being carried out of the Parish Church of St. Michael, which had been temporarily converted to a sick bay, corpses that were piled up on handcarts without any sort of covering—naked—and carried to the gates of the city for their eternal rest? In the church itself, more and more victims waited for aid below the archangel Michael, who slew the devil in the form of a dragon and in the process cast the devil down onto the earth. The remarkable organ melodies and the congregations' choral music had fallen silent.

In the last section of *The Phenomenology of Spirit*, Hegel wrote that "conceptually grasped history" was the "Golgotha of Absolute Spirit." While still the spirit in the form of the contingency of phenomenal existence, this "grasped history" was also the "science of phenomenal knowledge," a science for which his *Phenomenology of Spirit* had laid the methodological foundations. That was the philosophical narrative Hegel always bore in mind. No matter how many detours and byways history took at times, it was unfailingly governed by reason.

Hegel would not be able to stay in Jena, no matter what. What he now needed was a consistent livelihood. In Bamberg he might be able to get a job as an editor at a political newspaper. It would be worth spending part of the winter there even if he accomplished nothing more than incorporating the final revisions into the galleys and filling in text to replace any omissions. The manuscript was likely to have gotten jumbled on his way there, as though the sheets of paper were assorted lottery tickets. Friedrich Niethammer had found employment in the Bamberg school system; he could stay with Niethammer for a while. Somehow or other, Hegel would need to get back on his feet as soon as possible. He was running out of time. This war had many faces.

He was determined to write a letter to Niethammer and explain his situation. He would tell him about October 13, 1806, the day that the Prussian-Saxon army fled the city and cleared the way for the French troops. He would describe the eve of the Battle of Jena-Auerstedt, in which the Prussian army suffered a crushing defeat after the commander in chief, the Duke of Brunswick, Karl Wilhelm Ferdinand, a brother of the Dowager Duchess of Weimar, was blinded and mortally wounded by a musket ball and had to be carried away on a stretcher. He would write about the Döderlein House, which had been spared from the recurring fires in the city, and about the letter Goethe sent a few days later from Weimar to inquire how his friends in Jena were faring. The duke and duchess, Goethe reported, were doing well.

The beginning of the semester was postponed until further notice.

Life Paths

NOVALIS

The friend of the Jena circle died in 1801, but his works lived on. One year after Novalis's death in Weißenfels, Friedrich Schlegel and Ludwig Tieck compiled whatever they could: texts that were lying around, scattered about, passed over. They would issue an edition of the collected works, from *Hymns to the Night*, which was published during his lifetime, to *Heinrich von Ofterdingen*, the novel that remained a fragment. Schlegel and Tieck also took possession of the manuscript of the speech their colleague had given in Jena in November 1799 and decided to publish it in excerpts; it did not appear in full until a new edition of his writings was published in 1826. Novalis's work soon became known as the epitome of Romanticism, and the symbol of the blue flower, which had originated with him, emerged as the emblem of the quest for the infinite, which eludes us over and over again. In a disenchanted world, his call for reenchantment resonated ever more brightly.

AUGUST WILHELM SCHLEGEL

Wilhelm willingly remained in Germaine de Staël's employ until 1817—more than thirteen years, an endlessly long time. Luckily, his travels kept taking him out of the confines of Switzerland, to Vienna, Paris, Dresden, and Weimar. The translations of Dante, Cervantes, Calderón, and Shakespeare were progressing well. His bond with Madame de Staël lasted until her death. Wilhelm returned to teaching and became the first endowed professor of Indology in Germany at the newly established University of Bonn. Heinrich Heine attended his lectures on literature. Schlegel's translations of Shakespeare remain classics of modern literature to this day.

CAROLINE SCHELLING

When nothing else remained to her, Caroline was grateful that she was finally married to Schelling. She did not have an easy time of it in Würzburg and Munich, cities to which she unhesitatingly followed her husband. She continued to be subjected to social hostilities, and was known as "Frau Lucifer"; her past would simply not let go of her. Still, she and her husband did see Clemens Brentano again in Munich; Tieck was also there on occasion. But the Schellings' social circle remained small. On September 7, 1809, during a visit to Schelling's parents in Maulbronn, she suffered the same fate as her daughter, Auguste—she died of dysentery. Schelling was plunged into a profound existential crisis once again, but this time he did not emerge from it. The obelisks on Caroline's grave bear the inscription "Rest in peace, you pious soul, until we are reunited for eternity. May God, before whom you now stand, reward your love and loyalty, which are stronger than death." There are rifts that no amount of time can heal.

FRIEDRICH WILHELM
JOSEPH SCHELLING

Toward the end of 1803, Schelling left Jena. Maximilian Joseph, the prince-elector of Bavaria, wished to have him at the University of Würzburg. But Würzburg was no more than a passing phase, and in the spring of 1806, he switched over to the Bavarian civil service. Here he ran into an old acquaintance who had now become an outright foe: Friedrich Heinrich Jacobi, who, as the president of the Bavarian Academy of Sciences and Humanities in Munich, was his immediate superior. After Goethe had obstructed Schelling's reappointment to Jena in 1816, an honorary professorship brought him to Erlangen in 1821, before he was finally appointed to the newly founded Ludwig Maximilian University of Munich in 1827. The moment Schelling longed for came in 1841: He was offered the professorial chair that Hegel had held in Berlin. (Hegel had died in 1831.) Their relationship had also eventually developed into outright hostility, which made his gaining this position all the more gratifying. He was in high demand, and counted Søren Kierkegaard, Friedrich Engels, and Jacob Burckhardt among his audience members. But he would plummet from these soaring heights. Soon there were only a few scattered souls in the lecture hall. Schelling retired and died in 1854, at the age of seventy-nine, while undergoing spa treatments in Switzerland. No branch of philosophy was associated with his name, and he remained in Hegel's shadow. Eventually, Martin Heidegger rediscovered him as the German idealist who made the greatest strides in advancing a school of thinking beyond his own oeuvre. Today, Schelling's concept of nature is more timely than ever. The idea that nature has always been more than mere nature enhances our ability to interact with it in harmony.

DOROTHEA SCHLEGEL

In order to retain custody of her son, Dorothea had promised her ex-husband, Simon Veit, that she would not convert to Christianity. But as her marriage to Fritz in Paris in 1804 drew near, the time for conversion had arrived: Dorothea Veit, from a prominent Jewish family, became a Protestant, and only four years later a Catholic. She was just as committed to taking this step as Fritz, and held the belief that there could be no salvation outside the Christian faith. After the death of her husband in 1829 in Dresden, she and her son, who had become a prominent visual artist, moved to Frankfurt am Main, where Philipp Veit became the director of the Städel Museum. Dorothea died in the city of Frankfurt ten years later. As a writer and translator at the turn of the nineteenth century, she stood out among the prominent women who insisted on their right to self-determination and let nothing stand in their way.

FRIEDRICH "FRITZ" SCHLEGEL

When Fritz arrived in Paris, he sought contact with intellectual circles there. Soon he was giving lectures and immersing himself more and more deeply in language studies, primarily Persian and Sanskrit. This was an especially opportune time to do so, because Alexander Hamilton, a scholar of Sanskrit from England and an expert in the languages of India, was subletting an apartment right in their building. Fritz discovered the Orient for Europe, just as he had earlier discovered antiquity, and began to publish a journal called *Europa*. One day, when Sulpiz and Melchior Boisserée, the well-to-do sons of a merchant in Cologne, took lodgings with Dorothea and Fritz, the path to a new perspective was paved. These men from Cologne had such confidence in Fritz that they invited him to come to their city. Their only condition was that he marry Dorothea, who would have to convert to Christianity beforehand. Four days after Napoleon crowned himself emperor of the French in Notre-Dame, the conversion and wedding took place in secret. But Fritz's odyssey of the mind did not stop at this next stage in his life. In 1808, he and Dorothea moved on to Vienna, where he gave lectures on the philosophy of life. He died quite unexpectedly in 1829 after suffering a stroke in Dresden. Schlegel's theory of the novel revolutionized the discourse about literature, with the reader assuming the role of midwife whose ongoing critical self-reflection brings the text to life and continually reshapes it.

LUDWIG TIECK

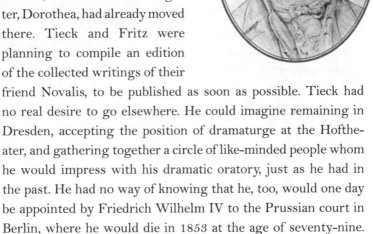

Before Fritz and Dorothea left Jena for Paris, they stopped off in Dresden. Ludwig Tieck, his wife, Amalie, and their little daughter, Dorothea, had already moved there. Tieck and Fritz were planning to compile an edition of the collected writings of their friend Novalis, to be published as soon as possible. Tieck had no real desire to go elsewhere. He could imagine remaining in Dresden, accepting the position of dramaturge at the Hoftheater, and gathering together a circle of like-minded people whom he would impress with his dramatic oratory, just as he had in the past. He had no way of knowing that he, too, would one day be appointed by Friedrich Wilhelm IV to the Prussian court in Berlin, where he would die in 1853 at the age of seventy-nine. What line had Tieck put in the mouth of Golo, the Count Palatine's majordomo, in his play *Genoveva?*

> Time passes by us, cold and indifferent; it knows nothing of our pain, nothing of our joys; it leads us deeper and deeper into the labyrinth, with an ice-cold hand, until finally abandoning us, and we look around and cannot fathom where we are.

Chronology

1775 Johann Wolfgang Goethe arrives in Weimar (November 7).

1781 Immanuel Kant's *Critique of Pure Reason* is published. The *Critique of Practical Reason* and the *Critique of Judgment* follow in 1788 and 1790.

1785 The *Allgemeine Literatur-Zeitung* is founded in Jena.

1789 Friedrich Schiller holds his inaugural lecture in Jena (May 26). In Paris, the storming of the Bastille heralds the beginning of the French Revolution (July 14).

1790 Friedrich Wilhelm Joseph Schelling enrolls at the University of Tübingen. At the Tübinger Stift he encounters Georg Friedrich Wilhelm Hegel and Friedrich Hölderlin.

1792 Beginning of the War of the First Coalition, with an alliance led by Prussia and Austria against France (April 20). Louis XVI is stripped of his office by the National Convention of France (September 21).

1793   The Republic of Mainz is declared (March 18). Two weeks later, Caroline Böhmer is arrested (April 2) and does not regain her freedom for three months (on July 5).

1794   Johann Gottlieb Fichte is appointed to the University of Jena.

1796   August Wilhelm Schlegel and Caroline Böhmer (now Caroline Schlegel) come to Jena when invited by Schiller.

1797   Friedrich Wilhelm III ascends the Prussian throne (November 16).

1798   February: Wilhelm Heinrich Wackenroder dies (13). France demolishes the Papal States and establishes the Roman Republic (15). May: The first issue of *Athenaeum* is published. Schelling comes to Jena for a visit at Whitsun and encounters Goethe and Schiller. June: Clemens Brentano enrolls at the University of Jena to study medicine. Schelling's "On the World Soul" is published. July: Wilhelm Schlegel and Schelling are appointed to the University of Jena. August: Friedrich Schlegel, Wilhelm and Caroline Schlegel, Schelling, Novalis, Fichte, and Johann Diederich Gries visit the picture gallery and the antiquities collection in Dresden. October: Schelling arrives in Jena (5). The renovated theater in Weimar reopens with the premiere of Schiller's *Wallenstein's Camp* (12). Schelling delivers his first lecture in Jena (18). The *Philosophisches Journal*, published by Fichte and Niethammer, is denounced on charges of atheism.

1799   January: The marriage of Dorothea Veit (née Mendelssohn) and Simon Veit ends in divorce (11). Schiller's *The Piccolomini* premieres in Weimar (30).

March: Schelling's *First Outline of a System of the Philosophy of Nature* is published. The War of the Second Coalition of an alliance led by Russia, Austria, and Great Britain against France begins (12). April: Fichte is dismissed from the university (1). Schiller's *Wallenstein's Death* premieres at the Weimar Hoftheater (20). May: Part One of Friedrich Schlegel's *Lucinde* is published. July: Fichte leaves Jena for Berlin (1). August: Pope Pius VI dies in Valence (29). September: Friedrich Schlegel arrives in Jena (2). October: Dorothea arrives in Jena with her son, Philipp (6). "The Song of the Bell" is published in the *Musen-Almanach*, edited by Schiller. Ludwig Tieck takes up residence in Jena with his family. November: Napoleon becomes First Consul of the French Republic (10). The Schlegel circle gathers on Leutragasse for group discussions of texts (11–15). December: Schiller moves from Jena to Weimar (3). Tieck recites his *Genoveva* drama to Goethe (5/6).

1800   April: Schelling's *System of Transcendental Idealism* is published. May: Schelling leaves Jena to offer a private lecture series in Bamberg (3). June: Schiller's *Mary Stuart* premieres at the Weimar Hoftheater (14). Napoleon attacks Austria and gains a decisive victory in the Battle of Marengo (14). The Tiecks depart Jena. July: Auguste Böhmer dies of dysentery while staying at the health spa in Bad Bocklet (12). August: Friedrich Schlegel is awarded his doctorate (23). The sixth and final issue of the *Athenaeum* is published. Novalis contracts a severe illness. Brentano leaves Jena. October: Schelling returns to

Jena from Bamberg (5). Friedrich Schlegel delivers his sample lecture (18). December: Goethe, Schiller, and Schelling celebrate the beginning of the new century in the house on Frauenplan.

1801   January: Hegel arrives in Jena. February: In Lunéville the peace agreement between France and the Holy Roman Empire is signed (9). March: Friedrich Schlegel's postdoctoral disputation takes place (14). Novalis dies in Weißenfels, in the presence of his brother Karl and his fiancée, Julie Charpentier (25). October: Wilhelm Schlegel holds his first lectures on literature and art in Berlin. December: Friedrich and Dorothea Schlegel leave Jena and head to Paris.

1802   The first issue is published of the *Kritisches Journal der Philosophie*, edited by Schelling and Hegel.

1803   The marriage of Wilhelm and Caroline Schlegel ends in divorce (May 17), Caroline and Schelling wed (June 26); at the end of the year Schelling is appointed to the University of Würzburg. Germaine de Staël departs France for a trip to Germany with Benjamin Constant (November 8).

1804   Wilhelm Schlegel leaves Berlin and travels to Switzerland with Madame de Staël. Napoleon appoints himself emperor of the French (May 18).

1806   French troops invade Jena (October 13). One day later, the Prussian and Saxon army suffers a crushing defeat at Jena and Auerstedt.

1807   Hegel's *Phenomenology of Spirit* is published.

Notes

A Philosophy Takes the Continent by Storm

8 *poem about nature*: Schelling published the scanty yield of this poetic endeavor in 1802 in the *Musen-Almanach*, edited by Wilhelm and Tieck, using the pseudonym Bonaventura.

8 *"true granite"*: Caroline wrote this to Fritz on October 14, 1798. Fritz replied, "But where will Schelling—the male granite—find his female granite counterpart? Would she have to be made of basalt at the very least?"

13 *later in the decade*: Carl Leonhard Reinhold in particular, who joined the Jena faculty in 1787, paved the way for the reception of Kant's work with the letters on Kantian philosophy he began writing in 1786.

14 *blue tailcoat*: Schiller's contemporaries described his outward appearance as falling somewhere between idiosyncratic and tasteless. Göritz, a tutor in Jena, noted that Schiller's clothing style gave "his whole physique a somewhat bizarre look, especially because of his knock knees and turned-out feet."

15 *collapse*: This occurred in 1792, during the New Year's celebrations hosted by the governor of the Electorate of Mainz. While recuperating in Rudolstadt, Schiller worked on his history of the Thirty Years' War, which laid the foundation for his later work on Wallenstein.

Venturing into Freedom

19 *Goethe would have loved*: In *Dichtung und Wahrheit*, Goethe wrote about his aspiration for his studies: "All my faith rested upon men like

Heyne, Michaelis, and some others; my most fervent wish was to sit
at their feet and attend to their teachings."

22 *"freedom flu"*: Georg Christoph Lichtenberg coined this term in a letter to Georg Forster dated September 30, 1790.

22 *on the military campaign*: Goethe sorted through his experiences of
his first campaign with the duke in his 1822 *Campaign in France*. This
text also contains the famous statement Goethe is said to have ut-
tered on the evening after the Cannonade of Valmy: "Here and today
a new epoch in world history has begun, and you can say that you
witnessed it." One day later, on September 21, 1792, the French Republic was proclaimed in Paris.

25 *butterflies fluttering over flowers*: One of the Prussian soldiers was
Lance Corporal Heinrich von Kleist, who was fifteen years old
at the time. In a letter to Adolphine von Werdeck dated July 28,
1801, he looked back on his military service in glowing terms: "My
heart melted as I came across so many inspiring impressions, my
spirit fluttering lustfully, like a butterfly over flowers fragrant with
honey."

25 *Forster's fear*: Forster voiced this concern in a letter to Christian Friedrich Voss dated December 21, 1792.

26 *Lucka*: Wilhelm contacted Georg Joachim Göschen, a Leipzig publisher, to arrange a place for Caroline to stay in Lucka. Since Wilhelm had to return to Amsterdam soon, Fritz visited Caroline several
times during her pregnancy.

27 *Döderlein House*: For a long time, Fichte's house—now a museum
dedicated to the literature of Early Romanticism—was incorrectly
thought to be the home of the Schlegels. For more on the confusion
surrounding the actual location of the house, see Peer Kösling, *Die
Familie der herrlich Verbannten. Die Frühromantiker in Jena. Anstöße–
Wohnungen–Geselligkeit* (Jena: Jenzig-Verlag Gabriele Köhler, 2010).

Best Regards, Your Outside World

31 *favorite gathering spot*: In the eighteenth century, student fraternities
had been formed on the model of Freemasons' lodges and were eyed
with suspicion by the authorities. All four of the principal ones—
Amicists, Constantists, Unitists, and Harmonists—were in Jena.
Even Fichte, who later distanced himself vehemently from fraternities, had been a member of the Harmonists as a student in Leipzig.

31   *academic freedom:* Because the "chocolatists" had reported forbidden duels, five Constantist students were expelled from the university in 1792.
Once riots erupted, ducal troops were sent to Jena on July 14, 1792. On
July 19, the students left the city in protest. The university backed down
and the troops withdrew.

32   *Red Tower:* The Red Tower was not literally red until 1870, when
natural stone was blended with red exposed brickwork.

32   *some ball:* On October 28, 1794, Schiller wrote to Goethe: "According
to spoken statements by Fichte . . . the I also creates by means of its
conceptions, and all of reality is solely in the I. To him, the world is
only a ball that the I has thrown and catches once again in the act of
reflection!! He actually framed his deity in these terms, as we recently
anticipated."

33   *theory of colors:* On February 19, 1829, Johann Peter Eckermann noted
down Goethe's remark "I give myself some credit for being the only
person in my century to know the truth in the difficult science of the
theory of colors, and hence I have an awareness of being superior to
many."

34   *intermaxillary bone:* Goethe claimed to have discovered it on March
27, 1784, together with Johann Christian Loder, in the tower of the
anatomy building in Jena. He wrote to Herder that same day, "I have
found—neither gold nor silver, but something that brings me inex-
pressible pleasure—the *os intermaxillare* in man! . . . It is like a cap-
stone for man."

Much Ado

39   *Stadtschloss:* The devastating fire in the castle on May 6, 1774, had
destroyed large portions of it, which is why Carl August considered
having a new building constructed (though he ultimately decided
against it). Thouret undertook the interior reconstruction.

41   *Magister Ubique:* This is also the name of a comic character in Ludwig Tieck's folktale novella *The Scarecrow* (1835). It first appeared
in a passage that can be read as an explicit allusion to the conditions in Jena and Weimar in 1800: "Everything is topsy-turvy . . .
Magister Ubique has his nose way up in the air, Ulf, the little law
clerk, gives himself airs with his poems even more than usual, Alexander, the young attorney, has been keeping himself away from our
company ever since, and my father is showing an interest in poetry
and literature . . . People in our circles are talking about sympathy

and antipathy, using phrases that no human ear has ever heard, they talk about progress, galvanism, and synchronism, which is enough to make your head spin."

45   *revisions to his prologue*: For more on this subject, see Norbert Oellers, "Goethes Anteil an Schillers Wallenstein," in *GoetheJahrbuch 2005* (Göttingen, 2006), 107–16.

The Dresden Pause for Artistic Effect

48   *"Athens for artists"*: Winckelmann's glorification of Dresden as a first-rate city for the arts allied with his notion that "imitating the ancients" was a benchmark of art. The idea of an aesthetics of genius, in accordance with Kant, signaled a radical break from this orientation to the ancients.

50   *count beans*: On September 21, 1796, Friedrich Schlegel wrote to Christian Gottfried Körner, with a reference to history rather than art: "It is odd how he [Fichte] hasn't the slightest inkling when it comes to anything that isn't about him.—The first time I had a conversation with him, he told me that he would rather count beans than study history. It would seem that as a whole, every branch of knowledge that has an object is alien to him."

The Most Beautiful Chaos

59   *Henry IV*: The translation was published in 1800 in the sixth part of the nine-volume Shakespeare edition, overseen by Wilhelm Schlegel. *Hamlet* was the first of his translations to be staged, and Wilhelm hoped to see *Henry IV* in the theater as well, with August Wilhelm Iffland as Falstaff.

61   *stung by a wasp*: Fritz had used this expression in an August 26, 1797, letter to Auguste in reference to Caroline. Now this expression could apply to him. Anyone who talked about Plato's bees had to count on being stung by a common wasp.

63   *"filthy nonsense"*: This was the way that Karl August Böttiger disparaged the novel. That "shameless hussy, Lucinde" in particular, along with the explicit public presentation of eroticism, had set him off.

66   *revolutionary mode*: One of the most astonishing declarations of this self-concept came from August Wilhelm Schlegel, who wrote to Elisabeth Wilhelmine van Nuys on September 13, 1799: "Imagine that all of German literature is in a revolutionary state, and that we, my brother, Tieck, Schelling, and several others constitute The

Mountain. We needn't be ashamed to participate, because the heads are . . . Goethe and Fichte."

The Imagined Subject

70   der dicke Lüderjahn: This popular name for Friedrich Wilhelm II came from his subjects, who considered him utterly unfit to weather the challenges posed by his era.

70   *freedom of the word*: Fritz even planned to write a pamphlet called *For Fichte. To the Germans.* However, the pamphlet remained an unpublished fragment.

76   *potential for riots*: The problem had started earlier on, in the 1794–1795 winter semester, with Fichte's decision to hold his public lecture series about the vocation of the scholar on Sundays during the prime hours of worship, which resulted in his being reported to the duke.

76   *smashed his windows*: Goethe described this action to Christian Gottlob Voigt on April 10, 1795. Böttiger wrote that Fichte did not venture out onto the street in the evening without a pistol after suffering an increasing number of violent attacks.

77   *the first notice*: On October 24, 1798, the publisher of the *Philosophisches Journal* announced that the issue had been shipped. On October 29, the supreme consistory in Dresden notified the elector of Saxony and asked for immediate confiscation of the issue. On December 18, the royal court in Weimar received a Saxon letter of requisition. Fichte had to defend himself to the sovereign.

77   *notorious Jacobin*: In his letter of defense, dated March 18, 1799, Fichte wrote, "It is not in my nature to make a secret of it . . . So I want to be the one to say the name of this thing. In their view, I'm a democrat, a Jacobin; that's how the thinking goes. When it comes to someone like that, you believe any atrocity without further evidence. Anything done to someone of this sort cannot be considered an injustice."

Helping Hands

81   *Luise, née von Hessen-Darmstadt*: Luise had been the wife of Duke Carl August von Sachsen-Weimar since October 3, 1775.

81   *"No hour strikes for the happy man"*: How quickly Schiller's lines came to be known by the public at large is also evident from the fact that this expression, still in common use today, did not even appear in Schiller's writings at all in this wording. He has Max Piccolomini,

who is head over heels in love with his cousin, Thekla, say: "Oh, he who has to count the hours / has already fallen from heaven / The clock does not strike for a happy man."

82 *"newfangled hot-air balloons"*: This term, coined by Christoph Martin Wieland, attests to the popularity of that technological innovation. In 1786, even Friedrich Nicolai, editor of the *Allgemeine Deutsche Bibliothek*, was forced to add a rubric to his journal on hot-air balloons. A wealth of information on this subject can be found in Rolf Denker, "Luftfahrt auf montgolfiersche Art in Goethes Dichten und Denken," in *Goethe. Viermonatsschrift der Goethe-Gesellschaft*, vol. 26 (1964), 181–98.

85 *financial situation*: It was essential for Goethe to stick to a detailed household budget, as he tended to live lavishly. During his first years in Weimar he occasionally spent more than twice his salary.

86 *loyal squire*: Goethe did indeed get Johann Jacob Ludwig Geist a civil service post. Geist left his position in 1804, and in 1814 he attained the coveted post of senior officer of the royal household and auditor.

89 *Wilhelm von Humboldt*: Humboldt lived in Jena from 1794 to 1797. He had been familiar with the region around the Saale valley since 1791, when he married Caroline von Dacheröden in Erfurt and spent the next two years on her family's estates in Thuringia.

90 *metamorphosis of plants*: Goethe described the scene in lively detail in his essay "Happy Event," which was published twenty-three years after this meeting (1817).

To Schlegel or to Be Schlegeled

94 *"To be or not to be—I or not-I"*: This quotation is from "Schlegels Monolog nach Erscheinung des Hyperboreischen Esels," in which the anonymous author pokes fun at Fritz's craving for originality.

96 *Willem Ferdinand Mogge Muilman*: Being educated by a philosopher worked out well for him; the thirteen-year-old son later became president of the Dutch Central Bank. He was no second Alexander the Great, but he did make something of himself.

96 *Rembrandt*: Since 1911, the portrait has been attributed to Ferdinand Bol.

100 *Sophie Mereau*: She was married to Friedrich Ernst Carl Mereau, a professor of law in Jena. Schiller, who recognized her talent early on, printed her poems in *Die Horen*.

100 *"wasps' nest"*: In the summer of 1798, Wilhelm had the first two issues of the *Athenaeum* sent to Goethe and tensely awaited a reaction
from Weimar. While Schiller sent a letter complaining that reading
it gave him "physical pain," Goethe was full of praise for the Schlegel
brothers and in his reply on July 25, 1798, he called these issues a
"wasps' nest" that set up a "fearful foe" to the mediocrity and the
"emptiness and lameness" of the other journals.

The Old Man from the Mountain

102 *contacted Weimar*: On July 24, Tieck, along with Wilhelm and Novalis,
was a guest of Goethe's in Weimar, and Goethe wrote to Schiller the
same day that Tieck "was, at first glance, quite a reasonable person."
Their lunch evidently pleased Goethe: "He spoke little, but well, and
made quite a good overall impression."

103 *Götz, Faust, Tasso*: This metamorphosis of characters was recorded
by Rudolf Köpke, who served Tieck in the same way that Johann
Peter Eckermann famously served Goethe. Köpke described Tieck's
first encounter with Goethe at the house on Frauenplan as follows:
"Goethe was actually standing before him. It was really him: Götz,
Faust, Tasso! But the sovereign in the kingdom of poetry, in all his
majesty, was also standing before him. A tremendous, staggering
feeling pervaded him at the very first sight."

103 *"reading machine"*: This was how Caroline described Tieck in a letter to Auguste on November 4, 1799. During his years in Dresden
(1819–1841), Tieck created an event out of his virtuoso oratorical
skills and gathered together a jovial social circle on a regular basis.

Intermezzo

110 *commencement of the new century*: Lichtenberg was predicting the future
with remarkable foresight. The number of planets did not quite double,
but the number of known large celestial bodies did rise from twenty-
two to thirty-one in the nineteenth century, and even though the air battles between the nations took a few more decades to occur, everything
listed here, far-fetched as it seemed in 1800, did generally prove true.

Vexing the Evangelists

123 *performance of Wilhelm's* Hamlet *translation*: It took place on October
15, 1799, at the Königliches Nationaltheater in Berlin, with August
Wilhelm Iffland in the leading role.

123 *worked until they were ready to drop*: The thorough cleaning had actually been completed in late September, that is, even before Dorothea arrived in Jena. The postponement to October could be explained by a tendency to procrastinate on such projects as long as possible, particularly in light of the fact that the "spring" cleaning had taken place in the fall.

Rulers Without a Realm

133 Kritisches Institut: Interestingly, Fritz and Wilhelm had just approached Fichte with the suggestion of founding a new journal. One day before Christmas Eve, Fichte composed a letter and presented a plan of action.

134 *rulers without a realm*: On January 16, a good three months after her arrival in Jena, Dorothea wrote a letter to Schleiermacher, describing their shared residence as a "republic full of despots."

134 *that Shakespeare passage*: The quoted passage was translated by Dorothea Tieck, the daughter of Ludwig Tieck, who at the time in question was just half a year old and presumably lay in a cozy basket near the fireplace.

Gardeners and Scholars

138 *"De officio philosophi"*: It was no coincidence that Schlegel's lecture bore the same title that Fichte had given to his first lecture; after all, he was determined to ascend to the Olympus of transcendental philosophy. The text of the lecture has unfortunately not been preserved.

143 *organ and document of philosophy*: The pivotal sixth section of Schelling's *System of Transcendental Idealism* states, "If aesthetic intuition is merely transcendental philosophy that has been rendered objective, it is self-evident that art is the only true and everlasting instrument and at the same time the document of philosophy that keeps authenticating anew, always and continually, what philosophy cannot present in external form, namely the unconscious element in acting and producing, and its original identity with the conscious."

145 *tombstone*: Caroline and Friedrich Schelling's wish to design a dignified memorial for Auguste stretched out into a lengthy process. Goethe, Tieck, Johann Gottfried Schadow, Johann Dominicus Fiorillo, Heinrich Meyer, and Bertel Thorvaldsen were all involved, but to this day a simple stone is the only marker at Auguste's grave.

Leaden Times

149 *divine sorrow:* Schelling would go on to present a detailed account of this particular state of mind as a principle of philosophy. The private lectures in Stuttgart (1810) stated that all of life had some element of an "indestructible melancholy," because there was something independent from it, inherent within it, yet posing an indissoluble contradiction to it.

151 *diehard editors:* Steffens's review was rejected with a reference to his status as a student and a reminder of the journal's policy not to accept contributions from students. In fact, Steffens had already been an assistant professor at the University of Kiel for quite some time.

152 *apartment of their own:* The exact location of the apartment was unknown until Johannes Korngiebel was able to determine it recently. It turns out to have been on the premises of the widow of Johann Wolfgang Bieglein, the fencing master in Jena, in the same house Hegel had lived in from July to October 1801, so Schlegel and he were next-door neighbors, albeit for just a few months. See Johannes Korngiebel, "Hegel und Schlegel in Jena. Zur philosophischen Konstellation zwischen Januar und November 1801," in Michael Forster, Johannes Korngiebel, and Klaus Vieweg, eds., *Idealismus und Romantik in Jena. Figuren und Konzepte zwischen 1794 und 1807* (Paderborn: Verlag Wilhelm Fink, 2018).

153 *One of the duelists:* The man in question was Leo von Seckendorff, who quarreled with a young French nobleman, Félix Du Manoir, at a court ball on December 18 for an apparently trivial reason and was severely injured in a duel the following morning.

153 *masquerade ball:* There are conflicting statements concerning the exact dates of when each festivity took place in Weimar. See Henrik Steffens, *Was ich erlebte. Aus der Erinnerung niedergeschrieben*, vol. 4 (Breslau: J. Max, 1840), p. 408; Norbert Oellers, "Allerlei Curiosa. Die Jahrhundertwende in Weimar vor 199 Jahren," in Marijan Bobinac, ed., *Literatur im Wandel. Festschrift für Viktor Žmegač zum 70. Geburtstag* (Zagreb: Zagreber Germanistische Beiträge, 1999), 5–24, esp. p. 21; Jürgen Beyer, "Die Veranstaltungsorte der Redouten in Weimar von 1770 bis 1835," in *Weimar-Jena. Die grosse Stadt* 8 (2015), 352–90; this passage is on p. 370ff.

Hegel and the Nutcrackers

159 *holding these sermons:* Most of the sermons were nothing more than tedious obligations, but at least in the case of Hegel's final sermon

there are early indications of central motifs in his later philosophy, addressing matters such as human freedom. For more on this subject, see Friedhelm Nicolin: "Verschlüsselte Losung. Hegels letzte Tübinger Predigt," in Annemarie Gethmann-Siefert, ed., *Philosophie und Poesie. Otto Pöggeler zum 60. Geburtstag*, vol. 1 (Stuttgart–Bad Cannstatt: Frommann-Holzboog, 1988), 367–99.

160 *page by page*: It is not certain whether Hölderlin, Hegel, or Schelling belonged to the Kant reading circle that was formed in 1790 in Tübingen. But it *is* certain that the circle soon broke up again. See Dieter Henrich, *Grundlegung aus dem Ich. Untersuchungen zur Vorgeschichte des Idealismus. Tübingen–Jena (1790–1794)*, 2 vols. (Frankfurt am Main: Suhrkamp, 2004), 716ff.

162 *spoke to no one*: The true reasons have yet to be clarified. Hölderlin had matriculated at the university on May 15, 1795, before suddenly taking off at the end of the month. In a letter to Schiller on July 23, 1795, Hölderlin admitted that the close proximity he had sought and needed had nonetheless deeply "disturbed" him.

Kant in Fifteen Minutes

173 *literary monument*: The anthology *Literarische Zustände und Zeitgenossen* was not published until 1838, three years after Böttiger's death, in an edition compiled by his son from his handwritten texts.

176 *Sophie Bernhardi*: When Wilhelm came to Berlin, he stayed with August Ferdinand Bernhardi, an old colleague at the *Athenaeum*. Bernhardi's marriage to Sophie was far from happy. Wilhelm seized the opportunity he saw here, and when Sophie became pregnant, she let Wilhelm think he was the father so that she would get support from him. The real father, however, was Karl Gregor Knorring, with whom she went to Dresden shortly afterward.

179 *The beautiful Tower of Babel*: In a letter dated September 11, 1814, Henrik Steffens wrote to Ludwig Tieck: "As certain as it is that the era in which Goethe and Fichte and Schelling and Schlegel, you, Novalis, Ritter, and I all shared a dream that we were all united, and we were rich in germs of new ideas, there was still something nefarious about the whole thing. An intellectual Tower of Babel ought to be constructed, one that all intellects can recognize from afar."

181 *"speculative Good Friday"*: Hegel used this formulation in his "Faith and Knowledge" essay, which was also published in the first issue of the second volume of the *Kritisches Journal*, dated July 1802.

Clearing New Ground

188 *setting the tone*: Caroline was not pleased to learn that parties were being thrown in her old residence. She wrote to Wilhelm on March 26–27, 1801: "I hope they told you about it in advance, yet I still find it less than tactful of Mad. Veit, as she was not driven to do so by necessity—they have a room in their apartment that is just as large—and as for the things they used, all the table linen and china, which had already been reduced so much by constant use, was my own odd little property, so in short, I don't want to hand it over at the next doctoral celebration."

194 Brotgelehrter . . . Universalgelehrter: Schiller introduced this distinction in his 1789 inaugural lecture in Jena.

The Night Before

199 *found a publisher*: After a dispute with Johann Friedrich Unger, which also stalled the Shakespeare project—the final volume was not published until 1810, after a nine-year hiatus—Wilhelm finally found a publisher in Berlin, Georg Andreas Reimer, for the Calderón translations, the first volume of which appeared in print in 1803.

200 *Frommann, the publisher*: As Hegel's postscript to his letter to Niethammer on October 13, 1806, revealed, he evidently spent the first night after the French invasion at the home of Commissioner Hellfeld. Johann Philipp Gabler wrote that Hegel briefly appeared at his home the next day before making his way to Frommann.

Bibliography

Anonymous. "Schlegels Monolog nach Erscheinung des Hyperboreischen Esels." In *Goldener Spiegel für Regenten und Schriftsteller*. Mainz: Vollmer, 1801, 103–104.

Anonymous. "Wann beginnt das neue Jahrhundert?" In *Der Bote aus Thüringen*. Schnepfenthal, 1800, 2–8.

Abeken, Rudolf. *Goethe in meinem Leben. Erinnerungen und Betrachtungen von Bernhard Rudolf Abeken*. Ed. Adolf Heuermann. Weimar: Böhlaus Nachfolger, 1904.

Bamberg, Claudia, and Cornelia Ilbrig. *Aufbruch ins romantische Universum. August Wilhelm Schlegel*. Frankfurt am Main: Göttinger Verlag der Kunst, 2017.

Böttiger, Karl August. "Ueber die erste Aufführung der Piccolomini auf dem Weimarischen Hof-Theater." In *Journal des Luxus und der Moden*, February 1799; rpt. in *Schiller und sein Kreis in der Kritik ihrer Zeit*. Ed. Oscar Fambach. Berlin: Akademie-Verlag, 1957, 434–40.

Campe, Elisabeth. *Aus dem Leben von Johann Diederich Gries. Nach seinen eigenen und den Briefen seiner Zeitgenossen*. Leipzig: F. A. Brockhaus, 1855.

Caroline: Briefe aus der Frühromantik. 2 vols. Ed. Georg Waitz. Leipzig: Insel Verlag, 1913.

Doebber, Adolf. *Lauchstädt und Weimar. Eine theatergeschichtliche Studie. Mit 20 Tafeln und Abbildungen im Text*. Berlin: Mittler, 1908.

Fichte, Johann Gottlieb. *Gesamtausgabe der Bayerischen Akademie der Wissenschaften*. I. *Werke*; II. *Nachgelassene Schriften*; III. *Briefe*; IV. *Kollegnachschriften*. Ed. Fichte-Kommission der Bayerischen Akademie der Wissenschaften. Stuttgart–Bad Cannstatt: Frommann-Holzboog, 1962–.

Förster, Eckart. *Die 25 Jahre der Philosophie. Eine systematische Rekonstruktion*. Frankfurt am Main: Vittorio Klostermann Verlag, 2011.

Frank, Manfred. *Einführung in die frühromantische Ästhetik*. Frankfurt am Main: Suhrkamp, 1989.

————. *"Unendliche Annäherung."* Die Anfänge der philosophischen Frühromantik. Frankfurt am Main: Suhrkamp, 1997.

Frommann, Friedrich Johannes. *Das Frommansche Haus und seine Freunde. Dritte durch einen Lebensabriss F. J. Frommanns aus der Feder Dr. Hermann Frommanns vermehrte Ausgabe.* Stuttgart: Friedrich Frommanns Verlag, 1889.

Gamper, Michael, and Helmut Hühn. *Was sind Ästhetische Eigenzeiten?* Hannover: Wehrhahn, 2014.

Goethe, Johann Wolfgang. *Goethes Werke.* Edited under the sponsorship of the Grand Duchess Sophie von Sachsen. 143 vols. Weimar: H. Böhlau, 1887–1919. Rpt. 1987, along with vols. 144–46, supplements, and index for the 4th division: *Briefe.* Ed. Paul Raabe. Vols. 1–3. Munich: Deutscher Taschenbuch Verlag, 1990.

Hartmann, Reinhold Julius. *Das Tübinger Stift. Ein Beitrag zur Geschichte des deutschen Geisteslebens.* Stuttgart: Strecker und Schröder, 1918.

Hegel, Georg Wilhelm Friedrich. *Gesammelte Werke, in Verbindung mit der Deutschen Forschungsgemeinschaft.* Ed. Nordrhein-Westfälische Akademie der Wissenschaften und der Künste. Hamburg: Felix Meiner Verlag, 1968–.

————. *Werke in zwanzig Bänden. Theorie-Werkausgabe.* Ed. Eva Moldenhauer and Karl-Markus Michel. Frankfurt am Main: Suhrkamp, 1969–.

Henrich, Dieter. *Grundlegung aus dem Ich. Untersuchungen zur Vorgeschichte des Idealismus. Tübingen–Jena (1790–1794).* 2 vols. Frankfurt am Main: Suhrkamp, 2004.

Hufeland, Christoph Wilhelm. *Leibarzt und Volkserzieher. Selbstbiographie von Christoph Wilhelm Hufeland.* Ed. and introd. Walter von Brunn. Stuttgart: Verlag Robert Lutz, 1937.

Hühn, Helmut, and Joachim Schiedermair, eds. *Europäische Romantik. Interdisziplinäre Perspektiven der Forschung.* Berlin: De Gruyter, 2015.

Jaeschke, Walter, ed. *Transzendentalphilosophie und Spekulation. Der Streit um die Gestalt einer ersten Philosophie (1799–1807).* Hamburg: Felix Meiner Verlag, 1993.

Kant, Immanuel. *Gesammelte Schriften.* Section I: *Werke* (vols. 1–9); Section II: *Briefwechsel* (vols. 10–13); Section III: *Nachlass* (vols. 14–23); Section IV: *Vorlesungen* (vols. 24–29). Ed. Berlin-Brandenburgische Akademie der Wissenschaften. Berlin: G. Reimer, 1900–.

Körner, Josef. *Romantiker und Klassiker. Die Brüder Schlegel in ihren Beziehungen zu Schiller und Goethe.* Berlin: Askan, 1924.

Koselleck, Reinhart. *Vergangene Zukunft. Zur Semantik geschichtlicher Zeiten.* Frankfurt am Main: Suhrkamp, 1989.

Kösling, Peer. *Die Familie der herrlich Verbannten. Die Frühromantiker in*

Jena. Anstöße–Wohnungen–Geselligkeit. Jena: Jenzig-Verlag Gabriele Köhler, 2010.

Krippendorf, Johann Adam. *Schilderungen der merkwürdigsten Kriegsbegeben-heiten bei Auerstädt. Von einem Augenzeugen und Führer des Herzogs von Braunschweig.* Apolda: Verlag der Thüringer Montagszeitung, 1808.

Lyncker, Carl Wilhelm Heinrich Freiherr von. *Ich diente am Weimarer Hof. Aufzeichnungen aus der Goethezeit.* Ed. Jürgen Lauchner. Cologne: Böhlau, 1997.

Müller, Gerhard, Klaus Ries, and Paul Ziche, eds. *Die Universität Jena. Tradition und Innovation um 1800.* Stuttgart: Franz Steiner, 2001.

Nicolai, Friedrich. *Beschreibung einer Reise durch Deutschland und die Schweiz, im Jahre 1781. Nebst Bemerkungen über Gelehrsamkeit, Industrie, Religion und Sitten.* Vol. 11. Berlin: n.p., 1796.

Petersdorff, Dirk von, and Ulrich Breuer, eds. *Das Jenaer Romantiker-treffen im November 1799. Ein Streitfall.* Paderborn: Verlag Ferdinand Schöningh, 2015.

Paul, Gertrud. *Die Schicksale der Stadt Jena und ihrer Umgebung in den Oktobertagen 1806. Nach den Quellen dargestellt.* Jena: Verlag von Gustav Fischer, 1920.

Paulus, Heinrich Eberhard Gottlob. *Entdeckungen über die Entdeckungen unserer neuesten Philosophen. Ein Panorama in fünfhalb Acten und einem Nachspiel.* Bremen: n.p., 1835.

Ratjen, Henning. *Johann Erich von Berger's Leben. Mit Andeutungen und Erinnerungen zu J. E. v. Berger's Leben.* Hamburg: n.p., 1835.

Rosa, Hartmut. *Beschleunigung. Die Veränderung der Zeitstruktur in der Moderne.* Frankfurt am Main: Suhrkamp, 2005.

Sandkaulen, Birgit. *Grund und Ursache. Die Vernunftkritik Jacobis.* Munich: Fink Verlag, 2000.

Schelling, Friedrich Wilhelm Joseph. *Sämmtliche Werke.* Section I: 10 vols. (= I–X); Section II: 4 vols. (= XI–XIV). Ed. Karl Friedrich August Schelling. Stuttgart: Frommann, 1856–.

———. *Historisch-kritische Ausgabe.* I. *Werke;* II. *Nachlass;* III. *Briefe.* Ed. Schelling-Kommission der Bayerischen Akademie der Wissenschaften. Stuttgart-Bad Cannstatt: Frommann-Holzboog, 1976–.

Schief, Walter. *Goethes Diener.* Berlin: Aufbau-Verlag, 1965.

Schierenberg, Karl-August. *"In Goethes Haus—in Goethes Hand." Goethe und seine Diener und Helfer.* Wetzlar: Wetzlarer Goethe Gesellschaft, 1994.

Schiller, Friedrich. *Schillers Werke.* Originally edited by Julius Petersen, editing continued by Lieselotte Blumenthal and Benno von Wiese. Weimar: Böhlau, 1943–.

Schlegel, Friedrich. *Kritische Friedrich-Schlegel-Ausgabe.* Ed. Ernst Behler, assisted by Jean-Jacques Anstett and Hans Eichner. Paderborn: Ferdinand Schöningh, 1958–.

See, Klaus von, and Helena Lissa Wiessner, eds. *Die Schlacht von Jena und die Plünderung Weimars im Oktober 1806.* Heidelberg: Universitätsverlag Winter, 2006.

Segebrecht, Wulf, ed. *Romantische Liebe und romantischer Tod. Über den Bamberger Aufenthalt von Caroline Schlegel, Auguste Böhmer, August Wilhelm Schlegel, und Friedrich Wilhelm Joseph Schelling im Jahre 1800.* Bamberg: Universität Bamberg Lehrst. f. Neuere deutsche Literaturwissenschaften, 2000.

Speyer, Karl Friedrich. *Dr. A. F. Marcus nach seinem Leben und Wirken geschildert von seinem Neffen Dr. Speyer und Dr. Marc. Nebst Krankheits-Geschichte, Leichenöffnung, neun Beilagen und dem vollkommen ähnlichen Bildnisse des Verstorbenen.* Bamberg: Kunz, 1817.

Steffens, Henrik. *Was ich erlebte. Aus der Erinnerung niedergeschrieben.* 4 vols. Breslau: J. Max, 1840.

Stoll, Adolf. *Der Maler Johann Friedrich August Tischbein und seine Familie. Ein Lebensbild nach den Aufzeichnungen seiner Tochter Caroline.* Stuttgart: Strecker und Schröder, 1923.

Tilliette, Xavier, ed. *Schelling im Spiegel seiner Zeitgenossen,* 2 vols. Turin: Bottega d'Erasmo, 1974/1981.

Waltershausen, H. G. *Der Diener seiner Exzellenz.* Stuttgart: Fleischhauer & Spohn, 1949.

Wolzogen, Caroline von. *Schillers Leben. Verfaßt aus Erinnerungen der Familie, seinen eigenen Briefen und den Nachrichten seines Freundes Körner.* Stuttgart: J. C. Cotta, 1830.

Zollinger, Max. "Das Schweizer Tagebuch von Goethes Famulus." *Neue Zürcher Zeitung,* October 18, 1931.

Index

Page numbers in *italics* refer to illustrations.

INDEX

ILLUSTRATION CREDITS

Frontispiece Franz Ludwig Güssefeld: Map of Jena and the surrounding area, 1:36 500, copperplate engraving, 1800. Photo: Klaus-Dieter Schumacher / Deutsche Fotothek

23 Richard Earlom, *The Plundering of the King's Cellar, Paris, August 10, 1793*: picture alliance / United Archives / WHA

44 Pieter Snayers, *The Battle of White Mountain*: akg-images / De Agostini Picture Lib. / A. Dagli Orti

51 Raphael, *Sistine Madonna*: picture alliance / dpa

68 Illustration from Guillaume Antoine Olivier's *Entomologie, ou, Histoire naturelle des insectes*: Olivier, G. A., *Entomologie, ou, Histoire naturelle des insectes: avec leurs caractères génériques et spécifiques, leur description, leur synonymie, et leur enluminée* / Coléoptères. Paris: De l'Imprimerie de Baudoin, 1789–1808

83 Contemporary depiction of the first flight of a hot-air balloon: Library of Congress / Science Source

106 Giulio Romano, *Olympus*: Scala / Art Resource, NY

117 Albrecht Dürer, *Nemesis*: akg-images

130 Friedrich Preller, *Skating at the Swan Lake Meadows*: Klassik-Stiftung Weimar

161 Illustration for Jean-Jacques Rousseau's *Discourse on the Origin and Basis of Inequality Among Men*: Library of Congress / Alamy Stock Photo

174 Louis Le Coeur, *Coronation of Napoleon*: akg-images / Laurent Lecat

193 Ore mining in Freiberg, Saxony: akg-images

205 Novalis: akg-images

206 August Wilhelm Schlegel: bpk Bildagentur / Goethe House and Museum, Frankfurt am Main, Germany / Lutz Braun / Art Resource, NY

206 Caroline Schelling: Art Collection 2 / Alamy Stock Photo

207 Friedrich Wilhelm Joseph Schelling: akg-images

208 Dorothea Schlegel: bpk Bildagentur / Nationalgalerie, Staatliche Museen, Berlin, Germany / Art Resource, NY

209 Friedrich "Fritz" Schlegel: akg-images

210 Ludwig Tieck: SZ Photo/Süddeutsche Zeitung Photo

A NOTE ABOUT THE AUTHOR

Peter Neumann studied philosophy, political science, and eco-
nomics in Jena and Copenhagen. He holds a PhD in philosophy and teaches at the University of Oldenburg, specializing in
German idealism. He is the author of two collections of poetry,
which have been awarded several prizes.

A NOTE ABOUT THE TRANSLATOR

Shelley Frisch's translations from the German—which include
biographies of Friedrich Nietzsche, Albert Einstein, Leonardo
da Vinci, Marlene Dietrich and Leni Riefenstahl (dual biogra-
phy), and Franz Kafka—have been awarded numerous translation prizes. She lives in Princeton, New Jersey.